Artistic Seed Bead JEWELRY

Ideas and techniques for original designs

Maggie Roschyk

KALMBACH BOOKS

Kalmbach Books
21027 Crossroads Circle
Waukesha, Wisconsin 53186
www.Kalmbach.com/Books

Eye For Color: Interchangeable Templates and Color Wheel System
(ISBN #978-0-9817161-0-7) image on p. 16 used with permission of
Gilbert Designs LLC.

Step-by-step photos by the author. All other photography by
William Zuback and James Forbes with these exceptions:
Mary Wohlgemuth: p. 2, 4, 5, 7, 9
Andre Tilin: p. 11 *top left*
Maggie Roschyk: p. 11 *top right and bottom left*, 17 *top right*
Gilad Rom: p. 11 *bottom right*
Jerry Visconti/Singaraja Imports: p. 45
Dreamstime: p. 17 *top left*, 49, 59
David Orr: p. 98, 99, 100, 101, 102 *top*, 103
Deone Jahnke/deonejahnke.com: p. 102 *bottom*, 111 *top*

Published in 2011
15 14 13 12 11   1 2 3 4 5

Manufactured in the United States of America

ISBN: 978-0-87116-429-2

Publisher's Cataloging-In-Publication Data
Roschyk, Maggie.
  Artistic seed bead jewelry : ideas and techniques for original designs /
Maggie Roschyk.
   p. : ill. (chiefly col.) ; cm.
  ISBN: 978-0-87116-429-2
  1. Jewelry making. 2. Beadwork. 3. Beadwork–Patterns. I. Title.
TT212 .R67 2011
739.27

Editor Mary Wohlgemuth
Art director Lisa Bergman
Illustrator Kellie Jaeger

Artistic
Seed
Bead
JEWELRY

This book is dedicated to all the beaders who have asked me,
"Where do you get your ideas?"

studio

contents

6   Welcome to My World

projects

30   Herculean Knot Bracelet

37   Blue Flame Pin

42   Poppy Pod Beaded Beads

48   Uroku Pendant Necklace

54   Banded Carnelians Necklace

58   Helena Elements

62   Stiletto Earrings

66   Art Deco Necklace

72   Intergalactic Love Song Necklace

78   African Turquoise Tubes Necklace

82   Easy Big-Sky Earrings

86   Urban Bedouin Cuff

91   End-of-Day Necklace & Earrings

98   Author's Gallery

105   Techniques Review

111   About the Author

welcome to my

What inspires you? It's an ongoing discussion in the creative world. Answers can vary from the grotesque to the celestial with everything in between.

Here's how it works for me. When I'm walking through the hushed halls of a museum or the wind-carved walls of a canyon, my senses are working, absorbing the surroundings. My mind records those images and impressions of paintings and sculptures, textures, and colors. The scent of creosote bushes after a rain in the desert becomes a memory. The texture of tooled leather on an old saddle resonates deep within me as if it were braille when I touch it. A display of iridescent butterfly wings in a natural history museum provides a never-ending well of ideas for color palettes.

I'm quite sure that you have had many of the same experiences, and those impressions can become part of your creative DNA.

My choice of creative expression is through beadwork. I've spent many, many hours chasing down tiny drops of glittering glass, pushing my needle through the hole, pulling the thread, and weaving the stitches. Through this precious craft, I've learned how to take my perceived impressions of things in the natural world and replicate the characteristics, whether colors, textures, or shapes.

I'm often asked, "Where do you get your ideas?" My answer is, "I observe and absorb my surroundings, taking notes along the way." My simple advice: Be open.

My goal with this book is to serve as a fire starter, and a friendly one at that—someone who can throw off some sparks to help you light your creative fire. This book is designed for intermediate artisans who have learned the basics of beadweaving and are looking to widen their vision of the craft. My goal is to send you, dear reader, on a personal journey to identify the things that you find beautiful or intriguing from your immediate surroundings, other cultures, or different worlds. Take those thoughts, impressions, and sketches, and, through the art of beadwork, make them uniquely yours.

The collection of ideas, thoughts, advice, and projects in this book can serve as a springboard. Use it on one level as a lesson book to help you finesse stitches and shapes. My hope is that as you develop as a bead artist, you nurture your own personal touchstones—your interpretation of impressions and observations of the things that surround you—as a great, creative well of never-ending inspiration.

world

home

My Tribe

What is the allure behind beadwork and all of those tiny, glittering seed beads?

Handicraft is expressed in many ways in all cultures. On a personal level, I've dabbled in and explored textile weaving, polymer clay, metal clay, wirework, and art glass. I've enjoyed the experiences that each medium has to offer, and yet I find myself drawn to the siren's song of glass seed beads. The tactile feel of beadwork, the never-ending possibilities for color combinations, the intricacy of stitches created hundreds of years ago and still in use today—these things always bring me back to seed beads.

There's also a soothing rhythm to beadwork: picking up a bead, passing the needle through it, and pulling the thread. This rhythm is familiar to me and it provides a hushed place that centers me, encouraging me to take on a gentle patience and quiet frame of mind. I must sit down and stop emailing, cleaning, dealing with all the details of each day. Beading can be exhilarating with its rush of new ideas. The sketchbook is brought out. Tubes and hanks of beads are aligned like actors waiting for their auditions. The needle is threaded and the thread is waxed; all part of the ritual before beginning. Hours fly by with the hundreds of stitches. When the last of the threads is trimmed, I am rewarded with a glittering prize.

I've often said that beading is like sitting down with a dear, old friend and having a wonderful conversation. Sometimes we talk about things in the past and revisit designs and stitches that I learned long ago. Other times, we talk about the future and the possibilities of color combinations and creating designs of our wildest dreams.

Through the experience of beading, we can develop a love for handicraft. The work and love devoted to each piece tells a story. Holding an intricate belt made by the Ndebele tribe connects me in some small way to ritual, traditions, and a culture that is continents away.

"It's all very tribal."
~ *Comment overheard in a disco during the '80s*

Through the ages, beadwork has been functional, signifying to others our tribal affiliation. In this era, our world is indeed quite a bit larger and yet, at the same time, made smaller thanks to information sharing and the Internet. Tribal lines become blurred. At any given time, I can choose to adorn myself with beadwork made with beads from Japan and the Czech Republic, a silver bracelet made in Mexico, earrings made with Karen Hill Tribes silver, and a ring made by a Hopi Native American silversmith.

Maybe my tribal affiliation should simply be ... human.

travel

Looking at Things

> People would say, "What do you do?" I'd say, "I make things."
> Now people say, "What do you do?" and I just say,
> ## "I look at things."
>
> ~*William Morris, glass artist*

The more I look at things, the easier it is to portray what I'm seeking to express in my beadwork. Here's something to consider: Which of the following would be the most compelling for you to look at? A mass-produced gold-and-diamond ring bought at the mall or an ancient gold band set with a hand-faceted stone that was unearthed in some ruin in Greece? For me, hands down, it's the ancient gold band. There's a story attached to that band, even if it's the story the viewer (or wearer) makes up in her own mind. I want to express that same feeling of creating a story or portraying an emotion in my chosen craft of beadwork—a way of conveying to others the things I saw while I was out looking around.

Years ago I sold a necklace to a lovely woman, who told me that she bought the necklace because the colors in the art glass bead and seed beads reminded her of plates and dishes that belonged to her mother. Each time she places the necklace around her neck and fastens the clasp, she revisits that sweet memory held deep in her heart. Knowing I'm able to evoke that kind of response as a result of the things I create touches my heart and makes what I do meaningful.

I hope this book will help you begin your own search for inspirations to use in designing beaded jewelry. Anyone with a basic knowledge of most bead stitches will have no problem following my instructions. (If you come across a stitch or technique that's unfamiliar, turn to p. 105 for a review.) Stitch away while I brief you on the many little decisions that go into a design as it takes shape. Sometimes I present a smaller or simpler version of the design or technique to make it easier for you to master. After that, you can approach larger and more complicated pieces if you choose.

An example would be the Stiletto Earrings and the Intergalactic Love Song Necklace, shown below. Both are made with cubic right-angle weave. The same stitch creates two totally different results.

Some projects demonstrate how choosing different bead colors will dramatically change the way a design looks. The Poppy Pods Beaded Beads (above) look graphic with a high-contrast black and ecru colorway. When stitched using patina greens and turquoise, the beaded beads blend and merge with the big Leland Blue Slag beads.

Feel free to use my color and bead choices as you're getting started; you'll learn and internalize my process. After you have made the projects in this book, it's my sincere desire that you will be well on your way down your own path—colorways and designs that make your heart sing.

I am passing on to you some of my guiding thoughts that I consider when designing beaded jewelry. It's my mission to provide simple and accurate instructions. I can only hope that my designs will be a jumping-off point for you to begin designing your own personal pieces.

Touchstones

What are your touchstones of inspiration for beadwork? They're all around you. Are you keeping a lookout for shapes and colors to feed your beadwork design ideas?

Most creative people have notebooks they fill with sketches and designs. If you're starting on a journey to explore and translate the things you love into jewelry designs, as I hope you are, I'd suggest carrying a notebook with you wherever you go to jot down notes and ideas. Take your camera along and snap pictures of things that interest you; even architecture and sculptures can provide lots of inspiration. Get lost in the stacks of art books in the reference section at the library. Do a little research on jewelry masters such as Cartier and read how fine jewelry is designed and constructed. All of these resources will feed your mind the next time you thread the bead needle.

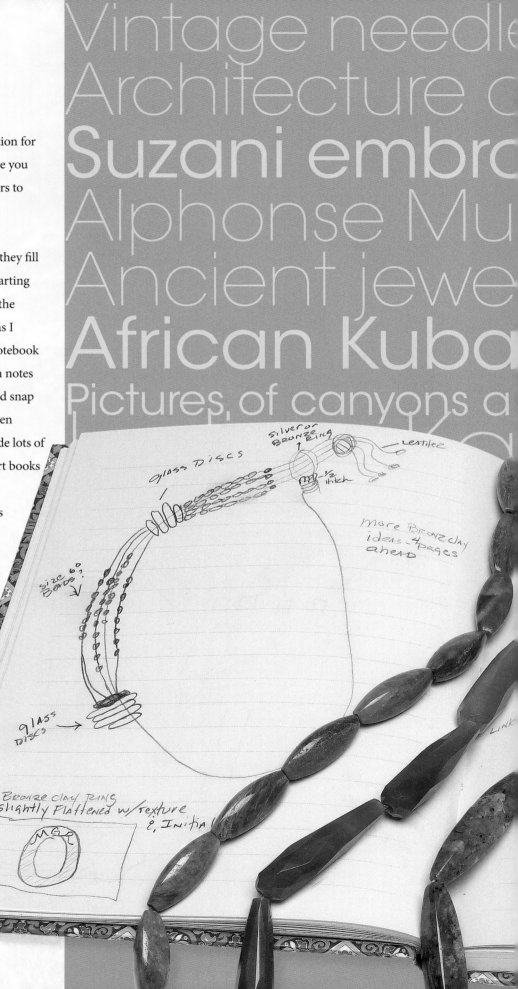

cover knots with plastic tubing these peyote tube

hanging from bottom down very visible

this could be just leather cords

monochromatic silver matte calc pearls

toggles

Embroidered with imbedded tubes for stringing stiff backing

ACTUAL COUNT

use metallic background? or flat black?

3 medallions

Choosing Bead Colors and Finishes

I've never taken any cooking classes. Despite that lack of training, my family and friends tell me that they love the food that I cook. I know what tastes good to me and am willing to try new flavors and spices as I encounter them. I apply that same mindset to creating color palettes for beaded jewelry. I have never taken a color theory class, nor have I read many books on color.

Choosing colors to use in beadwork, the way I experience it, is more of a gut feeling, intuition, or response. Often I tell students to choose colors that "make your mouth water." Many times beaders will put together a selection of beads based on preconceived notions of holiday themes, society norms, or colors that someone at a makeup counter said looked good on them—safe, but often uninteresting color combinations.

For example, the color-safe beader may look for springtime colors—pink, yellow, blue, and orange, choosing either all opaque or all shiny AB finishes (see below). Carefully stitched together, beadwork made with these colors may be technically good, but the work will be flat and uninteresting. In contrast, if one would choose an orchid pink seed bead, a pale cream, a muted gray-blue, and a burnished, gilt-lined shade of peach, the necklace might conjure hothouse flowers against a blue sky in April as the colors melt and merge. I might even toss in a sparing spritz of metallic coppery colors. It's the difference between wearing something ordinary or wearing a sunset around your neck.

I like to say "On the way to Color Town, don't stop at the carnival." Let's take a simple peyote-stitched band in which the designs or pattern is diamond shaped or even just stripes of three or four colors. Let's say the suggested color palette consists of blue, red, green, and yellow.

Color-safe choices and too many shiny finishes: a carnival of color

Extraordinary color choices in a range of finishes: Can you smell the hothouse flowers?

Often, beaders are tempted to go straight for the literal interpretation of bead colors and neglect to explore the myriad, and sometimes subtle, differences of bead colors, shades, finishes, and lusters that are available. The result? The beadwork ends up looking like something from a carnival. I would be more intrigued by beadwork made with neon shades (yes, there are neon-colored seed beads) rather than middle-of-the-road, timid colors or the obvious/easy choice of gaudy circus/carnival shades. Neon shades would a least convey a message of something contemporary—a pop art feel.

If your color choices are blue, red, green, and yellow, explore darker shades and lighter tints. Go organic with matte finishes. Go even deeper and look for earthy colors by picking matte metallic finishes. Add what I call an ethereal color by choosing something like a gilt-lined opal cream for the yellow. With careful choices, the peyote-stitched band can telegraph an antique look, bringing to mind Turkish rugs glimpsed in a crowded Marrakesh marketplace or hand-dyed wool being shaped into a traditional Navajo pattern on a timeworn loom.

So, you see, for me it's more than just making a blue and green necklace. It's about a feeling or a memory: how prickly pear cactus look in bright sunshine or the succulent shade of green with a faint bluish cast hovering on the surface of the cactus pads. While stitching away on the beadwork that evolves from that visual, I'll remember that feeling.

Are you looking for the inspirations that surround you?

What About Orange?

Beaders have strong opinions on the topic of orange beads. Orange beads often elicit comments about clashing colors and bad Halloween color combinations, but it doesn't have to be that way. Here's just one of many colorways that take orange from being a problem child to a beloved member of your seed bead family.

I started with a fabric swatch I loved. Fabric designers have already done the hard work for you, so you can easily base a color palette on colors you see in the fabric, paying close attention to the proportion of each color. I pulled out two tubes of orange seed beads, one opaque and the other matte silver-lined bead. I picked a complementary color of blue—its opposite on the color wheel. This smoky gray-blue tones down the outspoken orange. I added a dark rust and a matte, silver-lined gray to round out the selection. "Outlandish Orange" is now part of a sophisticated color scheme—not a hint of Halloween to be found.

I've never used a color wheel in my life. But after I pulled together this selection to share with you, a friend who's a beader as well as a quilter pointed out a color wheel tool that shows another way of looking at the color range that the fabric designer used and I interpreted in beads. See how the blue-gray lies opposite the toned-down orange? Complementary colors at work.

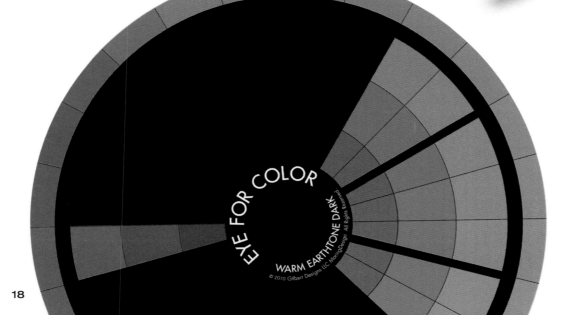

EYE FOR COLOR

WARM EARTHTONE DARK
© 2010 Gilbert Designs LLC MorningDesign All Rights Reserved

Auditioning Materials:
a Reactive/Subtractive Process

Why in the world would I include a quotation by an interior designer in a beading book? Read Darryl Carter's words on p. 19 carefully. Do you see how the creative process is at work, whether designing home interiors or creating beaded jewelry?

This quote sums up my color selection philosophy, especially when using focal beads or cabochons with seed beads. Some of the color choices have been made already. It's the beader's challenge to bring out the best in the focal bead or highlight the cabochon.

I consider starting a new beading project akin to hosting a small party on my beading tray. I'm going to gather together different and interesting characters and let them mingle. By carefully examining a focal art glass bead or stone cabochon, noting all of its different colors, I can identify the colors and finishes and then react to those colors. Contrasting seed bead colors might make a strong statement; the colors of the focal bead popping out

visually. If my focal bead is in muted, warm shades, I take care that the bead is not overwhelmed by shiny, gaudy colors of seed beads.

Let the party begin! I make a big pile of seed beads in tubes and various accent beads (below). This is the reactive part of the process. I always include a foundation color; a shade that will recede into the background and not compete with the focal bead. My pile of beads grows larger and the party is gaining momentum. I search for that ethereal color to include—seed beads in a tint that is lighter than the predominant colors of the focal bead. Beads that are gilt-lined or have an AB finish provide gorgeous highlights in beadwork and can supply that ethereal note, but use them sparingly.

Let's move on to the subtractive part of this equation. At this point, I have a big pile of seed bead tubes and accent beads representing many choices. Some of these choices have to leave the party; it's getting too large for interesting conversations to occur. The first beads to go will be colors that overwhelm the focal bead or cabochon. For example, the opaque green is too bright but the matte color-lined green blends in softly with the focal bead. Do the bluish purple seed beads clash with the reddish purple in the focal? If so, they're gone.

I eliminate colors until I have pared it down to an acceptable level of bead color ecstasy with two or three foundation colors, a burnished metallic color, and my ethereal seed bead tints. Everyone is now mingling well, I overhear spirited conversations—this party is good.

"Furnishing a room is like hosting a good party. **Gather together** different, interesting characters and let them mingle."

~Darryl Carter, interior designer

What's in My Beadwork Toolkit?

A beader is only as good as her (or his) tools. It's true. Someone can have an incredible eye for picking out beautiful bead palettes or come up with intricate bead patterns, but little beading can be created without tools. There's always some new tool being created for beading; some are truly innovative and make you scratch your head thinking, "Why didn't I think of that?" Here are the tools that I use and have found to be indispensable.

NEEDLES

Let's get right to the point, pun intended.

The most common bead needles are #10 and #12 longs. If you're stitching through backing material and leather, try #10 and #12 sharps – they're shorter and stronger.

Another needle that I can't bead without is the extra-long beading needle. These are primarily used for beading wide rows of loomwork, but I also use them for passing thread through long, tubular stone beads, like the ones used in Banded Carnelians.

Ease up on your grip. If your needles are bent, or breaking, it could be due to several reasons. Try not gripping the needle so tightly. When stitching very tight beadwork, try using a shorter length #12 sharps needle instead of the longer #12s.

Should needles have expiration dates? Does your needle resemble the letter C? Retire that needle; it's past its expiration date. Wrap it up in some paper and safely dispose of it. It's obviously worked very hard and now needs to go.

BEADING TINS

Tins make it easy to take your beading with you. Many craft stores sell small tins with lids that are perfect for making beadwork portable. I line my tins with a velour or Vellux bead mat. Don't use felt; its long fibers will catch the needle and cause beads to fling themselves into the dark recesses of the carpet. Glue down the bead mat along the edges so that beads won't hide under the bead mat.

I store a variety of needles in a repurposed mint tin that I glued some interesting handmade paper onto. Inside I have a stick-on magnet for any needles that are loose. (This is a good use for refrigerator magnets from the insurance company—simply glue them onto the inside of the lid.) Inside the lid is also my first son's kindergarten photo, wearing his Miami Vice T-shirt. Jacob's picture makes me smile every time I get a needle out of the tin.

PLIERS

Find some tiny chainnose pliers that will fit into a portable beading kit and on your beading tray. Be kind to your hands and use pliers to pull a needle through a tight bead. Pliers are essential for pulling needles through leather and Ultrasuede.

CALIPERS

Mechanical or digital calipers are excellent for measuring forms when precision is critical. You'll find these handy for a project such as the Poppy Pod Beaded Beads, in which I use wooden beads that need to be perfectly consistent in size.

SCISSORS AND LEASH

Scissors are easy to use and, at least in the midst of my creative chaos, usually hard to find. A leash keeps my scissors handy while I'm beading at home or teaching classes. My leash is functional, but that doesn't mean that it doesn't need flair. I strung my some of my favorite Czech beads and attached the strand to a Looplock, which easily opens to attach my scissors. It's available in nice metallic colors and helps me keep track of my scissors.

My toolkit contains three types of scissors. First you'll need a good pair with long, strong blades for cutting leather and foundation material. Then pick up an inexpensive pair of craft scissors for cutting the fishing line I love and recommend. Finally, a small, sharp scissors is very useful for making tiny cuts in backing material.

DOUBLE-SIDED TAPE

Every once in a while, you find a product that works consistently. I have used the various glues on the market for bead embroidery and, honestly, they're not my number-one choice. Double-sided tape from Therm O Web is my favorite: It's a no-mess, no-fuss way to bond everything together. My second choice is E6000 adhesive. Whichever product you choose, be sure to follow the manufacturer's instructions for best results.

PLASTIC

Bead artist Heidi Kummli gave me the idea of recycling plastic for use in beadwork. Clear plastic from annoyingly indestructible plastic packaging, plastic milk jugs … any stiff plastic can be used for bead embroidery. Sandwiched between the foundation material and the leather backing, clear plastic will give that extra stiffness and body to pins and pendants.

THREAD

The heavy hitters in my toolbox? Threads originally sold as fishing line: PowerPro and Fireline. Both are gel-spun polyethylene (GSP) threads. No stretch, no fraying, and nearly unbreakable. We spend countless hours creating our beadwork, so using thread that won't break is imperative. My favorite weight in the fishing lines is 8 lb. test and yes, you can thread it into a needle. (Tip: If you have trouble, flatten the thread end with chainnose pliers.)

PowerPro is a braided line that provides a wonderful drape in stitches like herringbone. It won't stretch, as nylon can. PowerPro can be used in all beadwork, even loomwork. My favorite color is a moss green so neutral that it recedes into the beadwork. Fireline, a fused line, is stiffer. Fireline works well when I want my beadwork to retain a shape. Most commonly found in a smoke color, it's perfect for beading with darker colored beads. An alternative to the smoke color is a semi-translucent color referred to as Crystal. It's a favorite of mine when beading with very light colors of beads. It's been my experience that knots are much less likely to occur with GSP and if they do, the coating on the lines prevents fraying. There's no need to stretch out the wavy kinks as you need to do with Nymo nylon thread. Despite all rumors and urban beading legends, these fishing lines do not disintegrate like regular fishing lines.

What thread is best for bead embroidery? Well, it's complicated. Because bead embroidery is supported by the foundation material and backing, and strength isn't an issue, I use Nymo in shorter lengths. PowerPro and Fireline are so strong that I worry they might pull too tightly on the foundation material.

WAX

I know what you're thinking. How can I possibly suggest using wax when I was just declaring the virtues of fishing line? I wax the GSP thread—yes, I do. If you are attempting to stitch beadwork that requires snug tension, you simply must try using microcrystalline wax. Get the real stuff from a bead store; don't try using candles or the beeswax from the fabric store. I divide my wax into several pieces—one for my bead tray and one for my portable beading kit.

MARKERS

Permanent markers are indispensable for changing the color of the GSP thread and coloring the backing fabric of bead embroidery. So many colors are now available; it's easy to match the foundation material to the seed beads.

TUBING

OK, I'll confess: Tubing is one of my secret weapons for beadwork. Is your tubular herringbone sagging and deflated? Line it with supple tubing and put some life back into your beadwork. Are you trying to incorporate an art glass bead into your creation but now it's clanking around on the thread? Line the hole of the bead with thin tubing and take the wear and tear off the thread.

For supporting tubular herringbone, look for tubing that isn't stiff; aeration tubing used in aquariums is rather stiff and won't drape. I've had great luck finding a variety of styles at hobby and model stores. Take along your beadwork or art glass bead in order to find the correct size.

LEATHER AND ULTRASUEDE

My favorite backing for bead embroidery is lambskin. I find this lightweight leather is easily sewn through using bead embroidery needles. Many leather stores can be found on the internet and if you're near a city with a garment district, there's sure to be a store specializing in leather.

I once found an entire lambskin hide marked $8 simply because there was a hole in the middle of the skin. It was dyed a gorgeous shade of metallic emerald green. Because

I use only small sections for lining cuff bracelets or backing pendants, it was perfect for my needs. If you prefer to use synthetic material as a substitute, Ultrasuede is available in a huge assortment of colors.

CORSAGE OR DRESSMAKERS PINS

Don't try to pick knots apart or remove stitches with beading needles. Keep a heavier pin—either a corsage or dressmakers pin—stabbed into your bead mat and use it gently on those errant stitches or nasty knots. Your beading needles will thank you and last a lot longer.

BENDABLE, FLEXIBLE RULER

My lil' beauty was found in the drafting section of an office supply store. Not only does it measure, it can also be used for drawing a template for a necklace since the ruler can bend and curve around the neck.

NOTEBOOK AND PEN

Why do I suggest keeping a small notebook and pen in your toolkit? It's quite simple. You're going to be so inspired from working on my projects that many new ideas will arise like butterflies. It's best to jot those ideas and beady dreams down before they're in flight and forgotten.

projects

Herculean Knot Bracelet

stitches
tubular herringbone,
even-count peyote, tubular peyote,
two-count ladder stitch

inspiration
Chinese silk textile

After reading this far, you know that one of my goals with this book is to help you shake things up a bit in your beadwork. From time to time, I feel the need to take some of my own medicine. All creative souls need to stretch, grow, and evolve.

Like you, I have my favorite bead colors. Turquoise Czech Picasso seed beads. Matte-finished, burnished gold charlottes. F463K 3mm cube beads (if you recognize this number as gold-green matte metallic iris, it's a safe bet that you have a similar affliction). These familiar faces are comfortable, but every once in a while, change is good. So how do we haul ourselves out of our comfort zones?

If you don't have an idea file to draw from, start one today. Get yourself a blank book, a pocket folder, or clear sleeves in a binder, and begin to fill your file with images and sketches of things you find interesting. For example, you may find a picture of an old cathedral window on the Internet and print it out, knowing that someday it will inspire a beautiful pendant. My hoard of ideas, collected over 20 years, includes a photo of a fantastic antique belt in the form of a Herculean knot, a concept that I knew would someday become a beaded piece. I got to work in earnest so I could include the project in this book. Day after day, as I worked out the design details at my beading table and searched for colors outside of my usual palette, the glowing colors of a Chinese silk weaving that hangs in my studio called to me. I was able to combine both inspirations into one bracelet.

I chose my colors carefully to suggest the weaving: glossy black, lizard green, opaque red with an AB finish, dark brass, and a metallic orange that hits just the right note. Fluid herringbone stitch creates a knot that's supple enough to encircle your wrist.

supplies

20 grams 11º cylinder beads, opaque black (color A)

10 grams 11º cylinder beads, opaque olive green with AB finish (color B)

10 grams 11º cylinder beads, dark gold (color C)

10 grams 11º cylinder beads, opaque red with AB finish (color D)

10 grams 11º cylinder beads, metallic orange (color E)

5 grams 15º seed beads, opaque black

2 4mm crystal bicones or rounds, black

Nymo nylon beading thread, size D, black

Beading needle, #10

Finished length: 8¼"

Supply note: In herringbone stitch, the thread is visible. Black Nymo is absolutely necessary for this project.

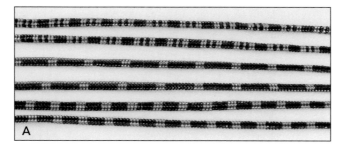

A

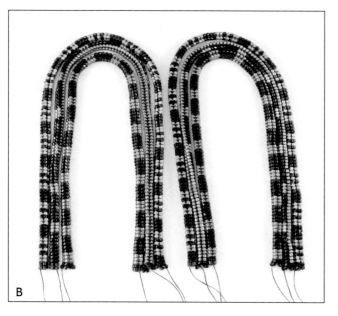

B

Let's begin by going over the beaded components needed for this bracelet:

1. A total of six ropes of four-count tubular herringbone stitch, two in each of the following lengths:
   • 10" (outer edge of knot, black and olive green)
   • 9¼" (middle section of knot, black, red, and dark gold; note that one side is dark gold and the other is black)
   • 8½" (inner section of knot, black and metallic orange)

2. Two even-count, flat peyote stitch strips for bracelet end caps [fig. 1]

3. One even-count, flat peyote stitch strip for toggle bar [fig. 2]

4. One tubular peyote stitch toggle ring in a triangle shape [fig. 3]

5. Two short sections of two-count ladder stitch for connecting clasp components to bracelet

Tubular herringbone ropes

Step 1 Begin by stitching the six four-count tubular herringbone ropes, which work up quickly. Keep the tension consistent so that the ropes are nice and even in appearance [photo A]. For each 10" rope, begin with a four-bead ladder of black (color-A) cylinders. Form the ladder into a ring and work the rope in tubular herringbone following a pattern of four rounds using As, two rounds of green (color-B) cylinders, a round of As, a round of Bs, a round of As, and two rounds of Bs.

For each 9¼" rope, begin with a ladder of two As and two dark gold (color-C) cylinders. Form a ring, then work a pattern in tubular herringbone: Work nine rounds with two As and two Cs per round, then work three rounds using red (color-D) cylinders for each stitch.

For each 8½" rope, begin with a ladder of four As. Form a ring, then work a pattern of five rounds of As and three rounds of orange (color-E) cylinders.

Step 2 Make two sets that contain one of each of the three lengths. Arrange each set in a U-shape with the 10" rope on the outside, the 9¼" rope in the middle, and the 8½" rope in the inside of the U. Place the strands closely together and smooth any twists, gaps, or overlaps [photo B].

Step 3 The ends of the ropes should be even. If one rope is longer than the other, adjust it by removing one round at a time until the rope is the right length.

Step 4 Use a square stitch thread path to sew the ends of the ropes together. You will end up with two flat, even U shapes.

Bracelet end caps

Step 1 On 3' of thread, work a strip of peyote as shown in the pattern [**fig. 1**].

Step 2 Wrap the peyote strip around the six-strand ends of a herringbone group to check the fit. The strands need to have enough room to lie flat and not crowd together. If there isn't enough length on the peyote strip, add 1 or 2 rows of black until the strip fits around the herringbone strands.

Step 3 Zip together the peyote strip. Don't trim the tail.

Step 4 Repeat steps 1–3 to make an end cap for the other group of ropes.

Step 5 Using the tail from a peyote end cap, sew through the beadwork to exit an **edge A** with the needle pointing toward the opening where the ropes will be inserted. Place the herringbone ropes approximately halfway into the end cap [**photo C**].

Step 6 Align the ropes so they are even, and start sewing the herringbone section into the end cap: Sew between two beads in a herringbone column. Sew under the thread bridge, and then sew into the next bead in the end cap [**photo D**]. Work around until all of the rope ends are securely attached to the end cap.

Step 7 Sew through the beadwork to the other end of the end cap, exiting at one end of the opening. To sew the end closed, pick up an A, and sew through the corresponding bead on the other side of the opening and the next bead. Repeat along the length of the opening. End the thread.

Step 8 Repeat steps 5–7 for the other set of herringbone ropes and the remaining end cap.

Peyote toggle bar

Step 1 Use even-count flat peyote stitch to work the bar half of the clasp: On 3' of thread, work a strip of peyote as shown in the pattern [**fig. 2**] using 11° cylinder beads.

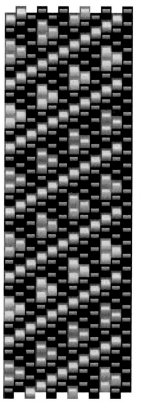

EDGE A
Insert ropes
on this side

fig. 1

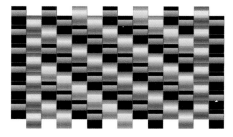

fig. 2

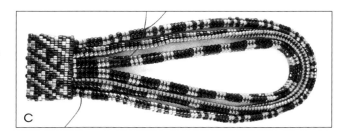

C

D

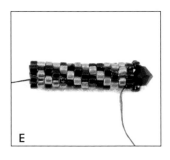

Step 2 Zip the ends together to form a tube. Don't trim the threads.

Step 3 Weave through the beadwork to exit an end bead.

Step 4 Pick up a 15º seed bead, a 4mm crystal, and a 15º. Sew down through the bead at the opposite side of the tube opening, and sew up through the adjacent bead.

Step 5 Pick up a 15º and sew through the crystal. Pick up a 15º and sew through the edge bead next to the one your thread exited in step 3. Reinforce the thread path several times to secure the crystal to the end of the tube **[photo E]**.

Step 6 Sew through the beadwork to exit the other end of the tube, and repeat steps 4 and 5 on the other end to complete the toggle bar.

Step 7 Sew through the beadwork to exit a bead in the center of the toggle bar. Pick up two As, and sew through two center beads in the toggle bar. Sew through all four beads again, exiting the two new As. Continue working in two-bead ladder stitch until you have a strip that is nine rows long.

Step 8 To attach the toggle bar to an end cap, sew down through a middle bead along the edge of the end cap. Pull snug, sew up through the adjacent bead in the end cap, and sew through the end two As of the ladder stitch section. Reinforce the thread path with another pass.

Step 9 To embellish the ladder stitch section, exit the pair of As closest to the end cap. Pick up a 15º, and sew through the next pair of As. Repeat along the length of the ladder stitch section. Repeat, going in the opposite direction, to fill the gaps **[photo F]**.

Peyote toggle ring

I wanted to play off the geometric patterns used in this bracelet, so instead of a round toggle ring, I stitched a ring with triangular points.

Step 1 On 3' of thread, pick up 30 15ºs. Slide the beads down to the middle of the thread. Sew through again to form a circle **[fig. 3, a–b]**.

Step 2 Working in tubular peyote stitch, work a round of 15ºs. Step up through two beads at the end of the round **[b–c]**.

Step 3 Work a round of As on each edge of the ring **[c–d and e–f]**. On one edge, work another round as follows: Work four stitches using one A per stitch **[fig. 4, a–b]**. Work one stitch with two 15ºs **[b–c]**. Repeat this five-stitch pattern twice, stepping up at the end of the round **[c–d]**. Repeat this round on the other edge, working the 15ºs in the corresponding stitches. The two edges should curve away from the initial ring of 15ºs.

Step 4 On one edge, work a round using A cylinders. When you get to a set of 15ºs, sew through the first 15º of the pair, pick up a cylinder, and sew through the next 15º **[fig. 5]**. Repeat this round on the other edge.

Step 5 Work one more round of A cylinders on the edge of the ring **[fig. 6]**. Press the edges together and zip them up, sewing through the alternating up-beads.

Step 6 Embellish the outer edge by adding a round of A cylinders along the outermost round. When you reach a corner, pick up a cylinder, a 15º, and a cylinder, and sew through the next cylinder in the round. Repeat around the entire ring **[fig. 7]**.

Step 7 Sew through the beadwork to exit the center cylinder on one edge. Pick up two cylinders and sew through two center beads of the outermost edge on the triangular ring. Circle through all four beads again.

Step 8 Work in two-bead ladder stitch for four more rows.

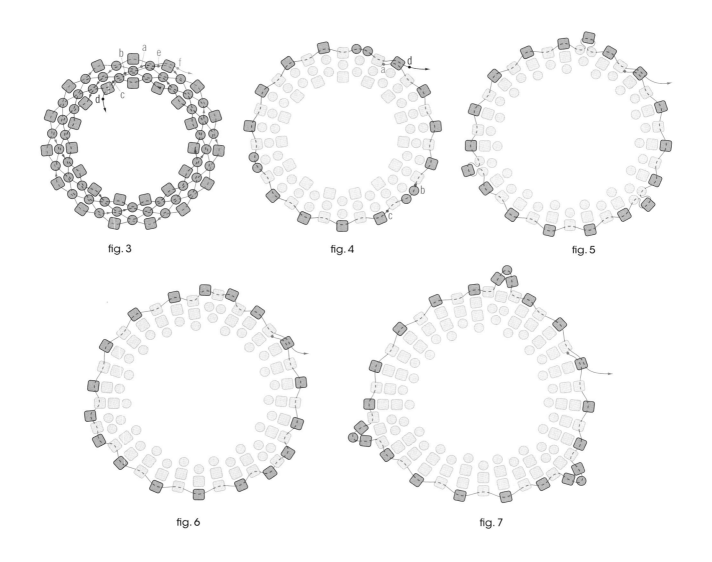

fig. 3

fig. 4

fig. 5

fig. 6

fig. 7

G

Step 9 Attach the remaining end cap as in step 8 of "Peyote toggle bar." Reinforce the thread path, then embellish the ladder stitch segment as in step 9 of "Peyote toggle bar" [photo G].

Finishing the bracelet

At this point, you have two separate beaded pieces—one with a toggle bar and another with a triangular toggle ring. Let's tie the knot!

Step 1 Place one beaded section flat with the toggle bar on the right. Position the other beaded section so the triangular toggle ring is on the left.

Step 2 Pass the curved ropes of the right section [photo H, curve A] through the opening in the left section [photo H, curve B]. Pass the toggle ring through curve A [photo I].

Step 3 Gently pull the toggle ring and the toggle bar in opposite directions [photo J]. At this point, the ropes will crowd each other. Straighten the ropes so they lie flat.

Step 4 Thread a needle with a comfortable length of thread and use a square stitch thread path to sew the straight sections of the ropes to each other where they intersect with the curves so each rope lies flat and in place [photo K]. To avoid pulling and straining the knot itself, stitch straight sections to the adjacent curved sections.

Step 5 End the thread and trim all thread tails.

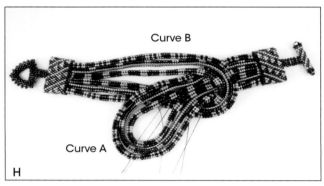

Curve B

Curve A

H

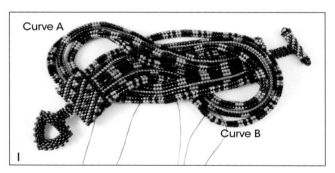

Curve A

Curve B

I

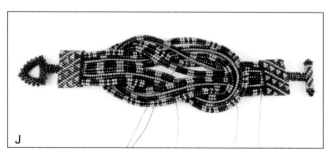

J

K

Blue Flame Pin

- -

technique/stitch
inkjet transfer, bead embroidery

inspiration
dichroic glass cabochon

*B*ead embroidery often begins with designs drawn onto a foundation material. In order to compensate for my less-than-stellar sketching skills, I've come up with some workarounds for adapting designs and applying them to the foundation.

Many office supply and craft stores carry inkjet transfer paper made for ironing computer-printed graphics onto T-shirts. This transfer paper enables you to use any design that you sketch, scan, or snag from a copyright-free clip-art site, full color and all! Print your design on the applique paper and then iron it onto your foundation material. Colors will be clear, lines will be sharp and crisp, and your design will be much easier to follow than if you used a permanent marker on the foundation material.

In this example, I wanted to create a pin around a beautiful triangular dichroic glass cabochon that a dear friend made for me. I'm often asked how I make color and bead choices, especially for a free-form piece like this pin. My simple answer usually is: "Play around with color and textures until you find something pleasing."

To give you an example of how I play, I'll take you step by step through my process for this pin (very typical of how I create bead-embroidered pieces). Along the way, you'll get ideas for applying my process to your favorite cabochons and accent beads.

Dichroic glass cabochons by Debbie Purdie

Preparing the design

Step 1 I find a rough idea from clip art designs and print it. The design needs a little bit of tweaking; I want to change the spirals, so I turn to trusty tracing paper, scissors, and a fine-point Sharpie marker to trace and then reposition the elements [photo A]. (I hope you'll be cheered to learn you don't need incredible graphic art skills or high-tech equipment to create appealing designs.)

Step 2 I place the dichro cab onto the design [photo B]. I darken the outlines and add some color suggestions to the background. (You can always change your mind later, but it's good to start thinking about color at this point.) I'm pleased with the design, so I scan it and save it in a format to use with my drawing or photo manipulation program. (If necessary, resize the design to fit your cabochon.)

Step 3 I print the design onto the applique paper and follow the appliqué manufacturer's instructions to iron the transfer onto the bead embroidery foundation material [photo C]. (This is so much easier than trying to draw onto the foundation with a permanent marker!)

Securing the cabochon

Beaders often use one of two products to adhere a cab onto the foundation material: E6000 glue or a double-sided adhesive tape like Therm O Web. I like both products; the key with either is to be sure no adhesive extends beyond the edge of cabochon because it is very hard to stitch through that stuff. I adhere the cab, leaving a narrow margin without adhesive around it. While I wait for the adhesive to cure, I look for beads to complement and bring to life the colors in the cab.

Adding beads

I'm not locked into using the colors I added to my foundation; they're just a starting point. I'll audition different accent beads, and we'll see which ones make the cut. I place my foundation piece on a neutral background, something like a white piece of paper or beige beading mat. I clear away any other distractions so that I can plainly see the piece. I turn on my iPod because listening to music helps me to "clear the mechanism," a great phrase I first heard in a Kevin Costner film about baseball, "For the Love of the Game."

supplies

Computer scanner (optional)

Drawing or photo manipulation software (optional)

Inkjet printer

Appliqué transfer paper

Foundation material

E6000 adhesive or double-sided tape (Therm O Web)

Iron

Beading thread

Pin-back finding

Backing fabric

Bead embroidery needle (also known as a sharp)

Beads: focal cabochon and assortment of pearls, crystals, seed beads, and semiprecious stone beads

Finished height: 4¼"

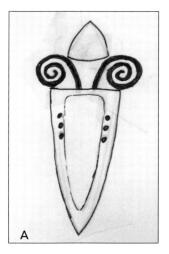

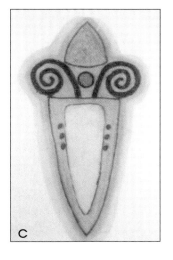

D

E

Taking cues from the dichroic cabochon, I begin selecting accent beads. The color of the dichro cab leads me down a jewel-toned path, which immediately brings peacock feathers to mind. (My mind frequently goes straight to peacocks and their intense finery!) I'll use my reactive/subtractive skills for choosing colors.

First up: pearls and crystals [photo D]. Intensity and saturated color are my criteria. The shapes of the pearls aren't that important; I know I can build around them with seed beads. I'm loving the round teal pearls and olive-green stick pearls. Looking at the crystals alongside the dichroic cab, it's easy to see how the flashy crystals can overwhelm a beaded piece. I want the crystal choices to enhance the cab, not compete with it, so I decide to use crystals sparingly. Tiny 3mm fuchsia crystals contrast nicely with the deep electric blues in the dichroic cabochon.

We've all heard the fashion advice, "Put on an entire outfit and then subtract one accessory." As you choose additional colors of beads, it's good advice. I want the intensity of the cabochon to be first and foremost, so my bead choices mustn't overpower it. I audition quite a few, including brushed gold Czech seed beads, metallic fuchsia cylinders, and several more pearls and crystals, but in the end I decide to echo the dichro cab by including a second, tiny dichro cab. I replace the teal pearls with a single deep fuchsia pearl. A stick pearl provides that bit of organic texture that I crave.

I settle for three colors of seed beads: the opaque black, a silky satin teal, and a blue zircon cut bead. Each color of bead has a different finish, which provides depth: The opaque black will disappear as it surrounds the cab and provides crisp outlines in the spiral. The satin-silky teal beads glow and radiate softly. I'll use the blue zircon cut beads only on the outer edge of the pin. They'll twinkle sweetly when the light hits them.

Start stitching

The dichroic cabochon has a base layer of black glass. I'll echo that by stitching the first row around the cabochon in beaded backstitch using black opaque 11º cylinder beads [photo E]. This first round should consist of an even number of beads surrounding the cabochon (I insist!). The next rounds are peyote stitched onto the first row with a step-up at the end of each round. Every cabochon is different, but for this piece, three rounds of even-count peyote stitch take the beads to the top edge of the cabochon. To surround the cabochon snugly, I stitch two rounds using opaque black 15º s, keeping the tension on the thread firm so the edge draws over the face of the cab. I sew through the last two rounds of 15º s a second time to strengthen and secure.

Stitching the background

Using the palette of three seed bead colors, I fill in the design using beaded backstitch. I start by stitching around the bezel with the satin-finish teal cylinders, inserting three 3mm fuchsia crystals on each side of the cab. I work the spirals above the cab with black 15º s and fill in around the spirals with teal cylinders [photo F]. I'm mindful of how the beads behave, making sure the beads don't pop up due to overcrowding. If the beading foundation shows through in spots, I use a permanent marker in a color that matches the beads to hide it.

I glue and sew a beautiful fuchsia pearl and the tiny dichro cab to the foundation and use black cylinders to begin a bezel around each in beaded backstitch. I stitch a round of peyote with cylinders and another round using 15º s. Three rounds of beads is enough—these smaller components don't need such high walls. After these accents are in place, I finish filling in the background, outlining the entire design with the blue zircon cut beads.

Final touches

After the design is filled with bead embroidery, I sew the olive stick pearl in place with several passes down through the bead embroidery and foundation and then up through the foundation and through the stick pearl again.

After taking a step back, I decide that the shiny black bezel around the large cab could use a touch of color. I sew through the beadwork to exit the second round of cylinders in the bezel. I pick up a fuchsia cylinder bead, and sew through the next cylinder in the round. Working in peyote using random complementary colors, I continue around the bezel until I've finished the round.

Now that the decorative part of my project is done, I cut around the entire piece with small, sharp scissors, leaving a margin of about ⅛" for a final round of stitches after the backing is applied. Don't get antsy and try to sew it on now!

Pin finding

I like to use a pin-back finding with a flat bar—it's perfect for sewing and gluing onto the foundation material. I mark where the pin should be applied, making sure the pin won't flop over when worn. For my piece, the best spot is near the top of my piece, under the swirling spirals. I glue and sew the finding onto the unfinished side of the bead embroidery.

Back it up!

Thin, kidskin leather and Ultrasuede are excellent backing fabrics. If you choose natural leather, be sure it's thin enough so a needle can pass through it easily. The pin finding needs to pass through two small holes in the backing. I make a paper template first: Measure the distance between the catch and the hinge, cut two small holes in the template, and check the fit before you cut into your nice backing fabric. Adjust the spacing if necessary and use the template to make cuts in your backing fabric. Slip the catch through one hole cut in the backing and the pin and hinge through the other. Press lightly and smooth out bumps.

To apply the backing to the bead embroidery, I use double-sided adhesive tape. Use the template to outline the shape onto the backing of the adhesive. Cut ¼" to the inside of that outline; the adhesive tape needs to be smaller than the

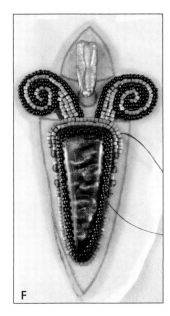

embroidery because it's very difficult to sew through and the edging stitches still need to be sewn. Apply the adhesive tape to the wrong side of the backing. Don't glue the nice side of the backing down! (Been there, done that.)

After the backing is smooth, press firmly so the adhesive can do its job. Using the edge of the foundation material as a guide, cut the backing material to the same shape [photo G].

Beaded edging

The pin needs a final round of edging. Thread the needle with about 3' of thread. Use thread that blends well with the backing and the seed beads used in the final round. Secure the thread to the edge of the backing by making several tiny stitches so that the thread won't pull out. Exit next to the last round of embroidery, pick up two cut beads, and sew down through the backing one bead's width away. Sew back through the second bead. Pick up a bead, sew down through the backing, and sew back through the bead just added. Repeat all the way around the beadwork.

Keep your thread tension consistent. After the last stitch has been made, sew between the rounds of bead embroidery to secure the end of the thread. Trim the tail closely.

Poppy Pods Beaded Beads

stitches
peyote stitch

inspiration
granulated metal beads

The notion of making a single bead out of many beads is very appealing to me. It brings Gestalt theory to beadwork: This whole is quite different than the sum of its parts.

Through the years, I've tried many different techniques for stitching beaded beads, always in search of the ideal way to showcase different patterns, colors, and textures in a smooth design without bumps or gaps in the beadwork. After much experimentation, I've finally developed a technique that satisfies my criteria. Give my peyote stitch Poppy Pods Beaded Beads a try, and you'll soon be addicted to making them, as I am.

Here are some important things to consider before starting your beaded beads. The wooden beads used for the core come from a chain craft store. They're reasonably inexpensive, but they're also inconsistent in size. Use your calipers to cull through the wooden beads, selecting only those that are exactly 16mm for this project. (Note that I used a 14mm wooden bead for the "small diamonds" version of this bead.)

I used Japanese 11°s and 15°s in black and ecru with black magatama drop beads as accents. Substitute any colors you desire, but keep the contrast high so the patterns really pop. I don't advise using Czech seed beads for this project because they are slightly smaller and will throw the proportions and bead counts off.

These five beaded beads are really versatile. All of the beads shown here are made following the same basic formula. The only difference is the pattern in which you pick up the beads and how they are embellished. For even more choices than those shown here, consider reversing the colors so what is dark in one bead becomes light in the next (and vice versa), or use more than two colors.

The first versions of the Poppy Pods I made directly mimic handmade gold granulated beads.

supplies (for one beaded bead)

14mm or 16mm wooden bead—unfinished or colored with
   paints or markers
1–2 grams 11º seed beads in one or two colors; matte black
   (color A), matte ecru (color B)
1–2 grams 15º seed beads in one or two colors; matte black
   (color A), matte ecru (color B)
18 or more 3–4mm drop beads or magatamas, matte black
Thread
Beading needle, #12
Microcrystalline wax
Calipers
Finished size: 16–18mm

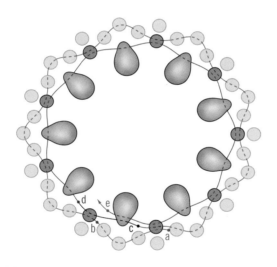

fig. 1

Basic bead

These beaded-bead beauties require 2–3 yd. of thread,
depending upon how much embellishment you want to add.
I suggest you use microcrystalline wax so your stitching stays
firm and doesn't slip around. You'll work part of the bead from
the equator to the pole using one end of the thread, and then
thread a needle on the other end and stitch up the rest of
the bead.

Step 1 Thread the needle and pick up 36 color-A 11º seed
beads. Center the beads on the thread, and tie the beads
into a ring with a square knot. These beads make up the first
two rounds.

Step 2 Sew through the first bead. Working in tubular peyote,
stitch three rounds with 11ºs. Maintain even tension—tight but
not too tight. Don't forget the two-bead step-up at the end of
each round.

Step 3 Insert the wooden bead into the peyote band to make
sure that it fits. Loose is better than too tight; you can always
tighten the peyote band by pulling both ends of thread. If the
tension is too tight, search though your core beads to find a
smaller one that will fit. Remove the wooden bead.

Step 4 Continue working in tubular peyote stitch using 11ºs for
a total of 10 rounds.

Step 5 Using 15ºs, stitch three rounds of peyote. Insert the
wooden bead. The decrease in bead sizes creates a smooth
gradation toward the end of the bead. Don't forget the two-
bead step-up at the end of each round. (I'm nagging, I know—
but it's easy to miss!)

Step 6 For the next round, work a stitch, and then sew through
the next two beads from the previous rounds **[fig. 1, a–b]**.
Repeat around. With each bead stitch, you'll sew through three
beads. At the end of the round, you'll sew through the three
beads and then a fourth for the step-up. You'll have nine peaks
around **[b–c]**.

Step 7 With your needle coming out of a peak, pick up a drop bead and sew through the 15º at the next peak [c–d]. Work around until you've added nine drops into the round. Step up by sewing through the last 15º and the next drop [d–e]. Keep an eye on your tension: It should be firm but not too tight.

Step 8 Pick up a 15º and sew through the next drop [fig. 2, a–b]. Push the 15º toward the hole in the wooden bead and keep the thread from looping around the drops. Repeat all the way around. At the end of the round, sew through the last drop and step up through the first 15º [b–c].

Step 9 Using 15º's, work in peyote stitch through this last round [c–d]. At the end of the row, sew through the last round several times for added strength. Don't cut the thread; it will be used for embellishment.

Step 10 Flip the beadwork over and place a needle on the other end of the thread.

Step 11 Repeat steps 5–9 to finish the second part of the bead.

The beaded beads can be embellished in a variety of ways. Using the long tail of thread at the polar ends, sew through to whichever round you would like to embellish. By "stitching in the ditch," you can stitch drop beads or 11º's into any round for more texture: Add one or more beads in each stitch or skip stitches, sewing through multiple beads to exit at the exact spot you want to add a little something extra. Use contrasting colors or bead shapes for visual interest.

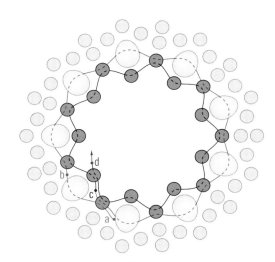

fig. 2

I think you'll find that these beaded beads are like eating chocolate chips—you can't stop at just one!—so enjoy making several with the additional patterns. I like to string them simply on a leather cord, interspersed with other favorite, bold beads to play up the graphic design of the peyote-stitched patterns.

Spiral-striped bead

Rounds 1–2: Pick up a repeating pattern of two A 11º's and two B 11º's until you have 36 beads. Tie the beads into a ring, and sew through the first A.

Round 3: Pick up a B, and sew through the next B. Pick up an A, and sew through the next A. Repeat these two stitches around.

Rounds 4–10: Work as in round 3, but in each round, begin with the color opposite the one you started the previous round with. Complete the bead as in steps 5–11 of the basic bead using color A only.

Connected diamonds bead

This bead has only nine rounds of 11ºs.

Rounds 1–2: Pick up a pattern of a B 11º and five A 11ºs six times.

Round 3: Work a stitch with a B. Work a pattern of a stitch with an A and two stitches with a B in each stitch five times. Finish the round with an A and a B.

Rounds 4–6: 18 Bs per round.

Round 7: Work a pattern of two Bs and an A six times.

Round 8: Work a pattern of a B and two As six times.

Round 9: 18 As.

Complete the bead as in steps 5–11 of the basic bead, but in step 5, work four rounds with 15ºs instead of three rounds. To add embellishment around the equator, work a "stitch in the ditch" in the middle of each diamond.

Small diamonds bead

For these beads, use 14mm core beads.

Rounds 1–2: 32 As.

Round 3: 16 As.

Round 4: Work a pattern of a B and three As four times.

Round 5: Work a stitch with a B. Work a pattern of two As and two Bs three times. Work two As and a B.

Round 6: Work a pattern of an A and B eight times.

Round 7: Work a pattern of two Bs and two As four times.

Round 8: Work a pattern of a B and three As four times.

Rounds 9–10: 16 As per round.

Complete the bead as in steps 5–11 of the basic bead.

Narrow band bead (only in teal necklace):

Rounds 1–2: 36 As.

Round 3: 18 As.

Rounds 4–7: 18 Bs per round.

Rounds 8–10: 18 As per round.

Complete the bead as in steps 5–11 of the basic bead.

The minute I saw a strand of Leland Blue Slag beads cut by lapidary Gary Wilson, I knew I had to create perfect seed-bead complements for them. Leland Blue Slag is a by-product of the foundries that smelted iron for the railroads in the 1800s; the waste product (blue glass mixed with borox and other chemicals) ended up in Lake Michigan as porous blue rock. Will I wear this enormous necklace? You bet I will!

Miranda's Maori hooks and incised beads

My 13-year-old daughter, Miranda, shares my passion for the art of craft. She loves to look at my books on old jewelry and had been re-creating Maori hooks with polymer clay. I showed her the Poppy Pod beads as I was working on them and mentioned that I needed simple round beads to place between them. She listened and then wandered off into another room, presumably to read (her other all-consuming passion).

I was busy beading and a few hours passed. When I went to check on what she was doing, lo and behold, she had been very busy using the same technique that she used on the Maori hooks, incising fine lines all over plain black polymer clay beads. I was so proud and grateful. Together we baked the clay and then wiped a creamy off-white acrylic paint into the lines. A little buffing on the legs of our blue jeans resulted in a group of beads with a timeworn, ethnic look—and a wonderful memory that we created together.

stitches
peyote stitch, brick stitch

inspiration
Japanese textiles

*Uroku Pendant
Necklace*

*D*eciding which stitch to use to achieve a certain result often challenges beaders. Let's say you find an incredible graphic with an Asian look that you would like to use for a flat panel in a beaded necklace or cuff. Peyote, loomwork, and square stitch all have straight sides and result in a flat, fabric-like piece of beadwork. Which stitch should you use?

Look at the inspiration textile or design. Does it have a majority of diagonal lines, 45-degree angles, or curving lines? Peyote stitch should be your stitch of choice. Do the lines sit at 90-degree angles? Try loomwork or square stitch. As you chart a pattern on graph paper, it will become obvious that some designs will work better with one stitch than another.

Uroku, the Japanese name for the pattern I used in this pendant, is translated as "fish scales." It is made of sets of opposing, contrasting triangles that represent dragon or sea serpent scales. I adapted this pattern for beading from *Snow, Wave, Pine: Traditional Patterns in Japanese Design* by Sadao Hibi and Motoji Niwa (Kodansha International, 2001). It fascinates me to know that this pattern can be found in other cultures, such as African art, as well.

supplies

Pendant

15 grams 11º cylinder beads, DB324 (color A)

15 grams 11º cylinders, DB352 (color B)

1 gram 11º cylinders, DB157AB (color C)

1 gram 15º seed beads for embellishment

Two 20–40mm art glass disks, one larger than the other

One flat keishi pearl

An assortment of pearls and semiprecious stone beads to complement the glass disks

Foundation material such as Lacy's Stiff Stuff

Leather or Ultrasuede backing

Beading needle, #10

Thread

Adhesive such as E6000 or Therm O Web

Finished size: 2⅝" wide by 2⅞" high

Necklace strap

Heavy beading wire (.024 or two strands of .018)

18–20mm art glass disk for clasp

Enough stone beads and ethnic-style silver spacer beads for your desired length

Crimp tubes or beads

Clasp

Crimping pliers

Wire cutters

Finished length: 22"

This pendant is a flat peyote panel with stacked art glass disks as a focal point. The pendant is embellished with pearls and semiprecious stone rondelles. The neck strap is minimal: gemstone beads, simply strung with silver spacer beads.

My color choices for the cylinder beads were driven by the colors in the art glass disks. If you cannot find art glass disks made by lampworkers, try using vintage buttons or anything lovely that is somewhat flat and can be sewn down. For embellishment, I chose pearls and turquoise rondelles because the colors were perfect for the subtle shifts of swirling blues and organic texture of the silver glass in the disks.

Part of the joy of beading is the incredible color combinations we can create. My cylinder bead choices needed to be subtle as well so the disks and embellishment wouldn't be overwhelmed. A matte blue-green cylinder with a slight patina provided a neutral color that complements and doesn't compete with the disks. An antique ivory was the perfect second color choice, lending a vintage look to the beadwork. My ethereal color choice was DB157AB. Mixed sparingly with the ivory, it provides a sly, subdued twinkle. Using this color alone in place of the ivory would have made the piece too flashy.

Stitch the peyote pattern

Step 1 Using peyote stitch, follow the pattern on p. 51 to bead a 2½" square base, stitching the wide body of the pendant first and then tapering the top and bottom by decreasing at the corners.

To create a diagonal taper, decrease along the edge: After completing a row, sew under the nearest thread bridge on the edge, and sew back through the previous two beads [figure]. Work across the row, and repeat the decrease on the other edge. In subsequent rows, the decrease turn is worked the same way, but will be placed within the previous rows instead of on the edge.

figure

Stitch the bail to the top. Don't trim the tail on the bail! It will be used for zipping the bail closed.

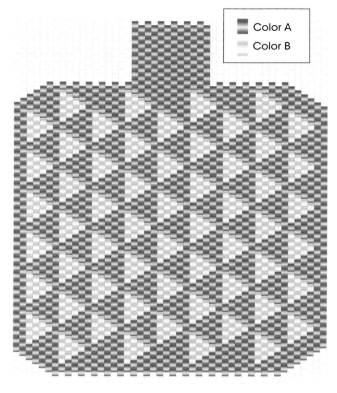

Color A
Color B

Step 2 Affix the beaded portion onto the foundation with glue or adhesive tape. Avoid applying adhesive near any area that will be stitched, such as in the center where the disks will be attached, around the rim of the disk beads where the embellishment beads will be added, and at the edges of the pendant where the edging will be attached. Apply the glue sparingly or attach adhesive tape in small sections. Following the manufacturer's instructions, let the adhesive cure. Trim the foundation material, leaving an extra 1/8–1/4" of material on all four sides.

Step 3 Of course, I like to audition different beads and pearls. Some will make the cut, some won't **[photos A and B]**. Try different layouts and be creative, but remember to step back and look at the layout, editing any beads or pearls that simply won't work in your creation. When you find a pleasing layout, take notes and perhaps make a sketch or snap a photo to help you recall bead placement.

pattern

Step 4 Glue the large disk to the base, aligning the middle of the beaded section with the hole in the disk. Use the smallest amount of glue possible and avoid getting glue into the hole. Align the holes and adhere the next disk and then the keishi pearl. Let the adhesive cure, making sure that the stack of discs doesn't shift out of place.

Step 5 After the glue sets, thread a needle with approximately 3′ of thread. Anchor the thread by taking a few small stitches into the foundation material on the back. Sew up through the foundation material, between beads in the peyote base, and up through the disks and the keishi pearl. Pick up a 15º, and sew back through the keishi pearl and the disks. Carefully sew through the peyote beaded section and the foundation materials. Pull the thread snug but not too taut. Repeat to reinforce the thread path. The disks are now secured by glue and thread, and it's time to start embellishing the perimeter.

Step 6 Take small stitches through the foundation material but not the beaded base until the thread exits the foundation material directly under the edge of the disk. Carefully sew through the foundation material and the peyote section, and pick up an embellishment bead and a 15º. Sew back through the embellishment bead, the beaded base, and the foundation material.

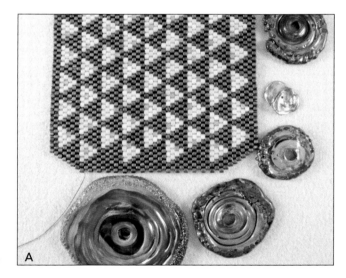

A

B

C

Step 7 Continue sewing down the embellishment beads along the perimeter of the large disk [photo C]. Take a moment to review your design. Don't overdo the embellishment; the beautiful peyote-stitched pattern shouldn't be totally obscured.

Apply the backing

The tab at the top of the pendant will be zipped up to form a tube bail, which will allow the pendant to be securely strung on a beaded strap. The leather backing doesn't extend into the bail.

Step 1 Apply adhesive to the back of the foundation material, keeping it ¼" away from the edge. Press the glued side of the foundation onto the wrong side of the backing fabric, smoothing out any bumps or wrinkles. Let the adhesive cure and then trim the backing even with the foundation material.

Step 2 Zip the end row of the tab to the base row of the tab to form a tube. Sew back through the zipped portion to reinforce. This is an excellent place to pause and use a permanent marker to darken the raw edge of the foundation material. If possible, use a marker that matches the color of the beads along the edge of the peyote base or the leather backing.

Stitch the edging

Step 1 Thread the needle with 3' of thread. It's easier to use a single thread to start and finish the edging rather than ending and adding more thread. Pass the needle between the leather backing and the foundation, and sew up through the foundation material. Make several tiny stitches in the foundation material to lock in the thread, exiting near the top edge of the beadwork. Tuck the tail of the thread between the leather backing and foundation material.

Step 2 Pick up two color-A cylinder beads and sew down through the foundation material and backing approximately one bead away from where the thread is exiting. Pull gently. Check to be sure the cylinders are standing on their ends and not on their sides. Sew back through the second cylinder and pull gently. Pick up a cylinder and sew down through all layers approximately one bead away from the last bead. Pull gently and then sew back up through that last bead. This type of brick stitch edging not only seams together the edge of the foundation material and the backing but also binds the edges against fraying. Keep brick stitching the edge until you come to the bail. Stitch the edge of the foundation material and the leather backing straight across, parallel to the zipped portion of the bail. Use tiny stitches. At the edge of the bail, return to brick stitching the edging until the last bead meets the first bead, and join the two beads. Sew through the foundation material and up through a part of the peyote base along the edge. Carefully sew through some of the peyote base beads and pull gently so the thread disappears into the beadwork. Repeat until the thread is embedded into the peyote stitching. Trim the thread.

String the neck strap

Lay out your design for the neck strap on your table or beading board. Keep it simple; the Uroku pendant is the star of the show. String half of the length of the neck strap onto a beading wire and pass the wire through the pendant bail. Continue stringing the strap on the other side of the pendant until you reach the desired length. Attach the clasp using crimp beads.

Put the necklace around your neck and run to the mirror . . .
admire yourself!

Loomed
Greek Key cuff

I made this cuff bracelet in a similar way. Work the pattern
provided in loomwork instead of peyote and attach the
embellishment beads. Sandwich the bracelet blank between
the foundation and the backing, and stitch the edging as you
did for the Uroku Pendant.

Banded Carnelians Necklace

stitches
modified herringbone stitch

inspiration
Ashanti brass beads

*I*t's no surprise that one of my favorite pastimes is going to bead shows. I love seeing colors and finishes of seed beads in person, of course, but I also seek out ethnic or vintage beads. Not long ago, I purchased an assortment of Ashanti brass beads that are handmade in Ghana with a centuries-old, lost-wax casting process. I'm totally enamored of the look and feel of these beads, and my collection became an inspiration that I wanted to portray in seed beads.

I also seek out unusual gemstone beads as I travel. Long, faceted stone beads like these carnelians are lovely to behold, but sadly and inevitably, there will be some beads in a strand that have flaws or poor color. It seems like a shame to waste these less-than-excellent beads. My Ashanti bead inspiration led me to the idea of stitching frames or bands that camouflage the flaws and yet don't completely cover the stone bead.

The stitch I used to bind the carnelians is one that I've been using for quite some time, more akin to herringbone stitch rather than square stitch. I use it for connecting beaded toggles to the main portion of a beaded necklace or bracelet. To my eye, it reminds me of a type of cording, and its strength is perfect for attaching one component to another.

supplies

16" strand 27–35mm tubular carnelian beads

5 10mm melon-shaped carnelian beads

25x50mm drop-shaped carnelian bead

1 gram 8º seed beads

1 gram 11º seed beads

20–25 grams 11º cylinder beads

5 grams 15º seed beads

49 3mm Swarovski sequins for embellishment

8mm spacer

9 6mm bead caps

8mm bead cap

Fireline, 6 lb. test

Beading needle, #12

Flexible beading wire, .024

Clasp

4 crimp beads

2 wire guards

4 crimp covers

Crimping pliers

Wire cutters

Finished length: 23" plus 3" pendant drop

Each of these banded beads will take more thread than normal. To alleviate dealing with an extra-long thread, start the beadwork in the middle of a 3' length of thread and leave a long tail. Wind the tail around an index card and tape it down.

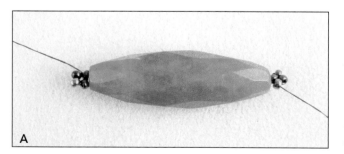

A

Stitch a base at each end of a stone bead

Step 1 Pick up four 11º seed beads. Sew through all four beads to form a ring. Think of these beads as the points of a compass: North, South, East, and West. The needle is now exiting the North bead.

Step 2 Sew through a stone bead.

Step 3 Pick up four 11º seed beads. Sew through these four beads to form a ring. Slide the ring down to the opening of the stone bead [photo A]. Don't leave a big gap between the stone bead and the ring of 11ºs.

Step 4 With the needle exiting the North bead, sew back down through the stone bead. Sew through the South bead of the original ring of beads. Now you have a base on each end of the stone bead.

Step 5 Sew back through the stone bead, through the South bead, and back through the stone bead. The bases should be firmly seated at the ends of the stone bead. If necessary, tighten the rings to the stone bead by sewing up and down through the stone bead and sewing through the East and West beads.

Beaded bands

Step 1 With the needle exiting an 11º on one end of the stone bead, pick up two 11º cylinders. Sew through the original 11º compass seed bead in the base, continue through the next cylinder, and pull snug. Remember that this stitch resembles herringbone stitch, so the beads will line up in columns that are two beads wide, with the holes running vertically and not horizontally.

Step 2 Pick up two 11º cylinders. Sew down through one cylinder from the previous row and up through the adjacent cylinder and the new cylinder above it.

Step 3 Repeat step 2 until the segment is long enough to attach to the base beads on the opposite end of the stone bead. For my stone beads, I stitched 26 rows. Your stone beads may be longer or shorter, so adjust the length of the band to fit.

Step 4 When the band is long enough to reach an 11º seed bead on the opposite end of the stone bead, sew through an 11º, back down through an 11º cylinder, and up through the adjacent 11º cylinder [photo B].

Step 5 Sew back through the adjacent cylinder and 11º, and then continue through the next 11º in the base. Think of it as sewing from a North bead to a West bead.

Step 6 Work another band by repeating steps 1–5. Repeat until you have four bands surrounding the stone bead.

Step 7 To connect the vertical bands with horizontal bands, sew through a band to exit the middle two rows. Since I had 26 rows, I will start my horizontal band on rows 13 and 14. Pick up two 11º cylinders, and sew through the two middle beads on the vertical band [photo C], then sew through the first cylinder just added. Work a band off of the two new beads that is long enough to reach the next vertical band, and sew through the middle two beads. Repeat around the stone bead to make a horizontal band the encircles the stone.

Step 8 Sew through the beadwork to exit in the middle of a four-bead intersection. Pick up a 3mm crystal sequin and a 15º seed bead. Sew back through the sequin [photo D] and sew through the beadwork to exit the next intersection. Repeat around.

Step 9 Make a total of six banded beads.

Pendant

Work the pendant in the same manner as the banded beads with the following changes:
• Begin with a ring of five 11º seed beads at each end of the pendant bead.
• Work enough rows to span the pendant bead (about 40).
• Make five vertical bands instead of four.
• Connect the vertical bands with three horizontal bands—one near the bottom and two near the top.

A few variations beaded around crystals.

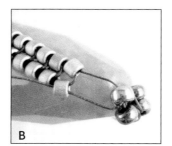
B

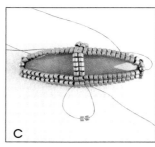
C

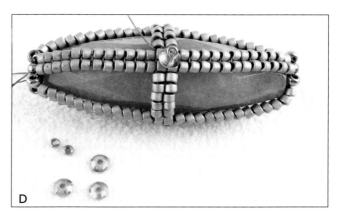
D

Necklace

Step 1 Cut about 30" of flexible beading wire, and center an 11º seed bead.

Step 2 Over both ends, string a 6mm bead cap, the pendant bead, an 8mm spacer, a 10mm melon bead, and an 8mm bead cap.

Step 3 Separate the wires and, on each, string a pattern of an 8º seed bead, an unembellished 27–35mm carnelian bead, an 8º, and a banded bead three times. On each end, string an 8º, an unbanded bead, an 8º, a 6mm bead cap, a melon bead, a 6mm bead cap, an 8º, an unbanded bead, an 8º, a crimp bead, a 6mm bead cap, a melon bead, a 6mm bead cap, a crimp bead, an 8º, and one side of a wire guard. String a clasp into the wire guard, then guide the beading wire through the other side of the wire guard and back through the last five beads and bead caps strung. Crimp the crimp beads, and cover the crimp beads with crimp covers.

Helena Elements

stitches
right-angle weave, peyote stitch

inspiration
ancient Mediterranean jewelry

Sometimes necessity can be the mother of invention. I purchased a strand of 8mm amazonite cubes not long ago. I was drawn by the pale blue color; it's a slightly different hue for me, not the green-blue of my beloved turquoise. I took the strand home from the bead show and did what any bead fanatic does: I placed them on my beading table, within easy view so the ideas could start percolating.

Simply stringing these beauties was too easy. As you may notice after paging through this book, I am rather obsessed with beading small components and building onto those components to make something larger. These cubes were perfect for this approach: I designed a setting that is beautiful and adaptable. The Helena Elements are quick and easy to make; you use only two stitches—right-angle weave and two rows of peyote that create a bezel around each cube.

And what about color palette? I find great inspiration in jewelry of antiquity, so I envisioned pairing the pale blue of the amazonite with burnished old gold as in an ancient Mediterranean treasure.

Consider these little cubes of beady goodness as building blocks, the foundation for constructing bigger jewelry. Turn one Helena Element into a ring by stitching a simple ladder-stitched band. Attach a drop or briolette on one point and a loop for an earring wire on another, and the element becomes an earring. Feeling ambitious? Since these elements work up rather quickly, you can stitch up a cuff bracelet or elegant necklace in a reasonable time. I urge you to bead a lot of Helena Elements and piece them together into whatever shape your imagination dreams up.

supplies (for one element)

8mm semiprecious stone cube, center drilled

1–2 grams 11º seed beads, F460R (color A)

1–2 grams 11º seed beads, pale turquoise matte color lined
 (color B)

1 gram 15º seed beads, opaque turquoise (color C)

4 3–4mm magatamas or drops

Power Pro, 8-lb. test

Beading needle, #12

Microcrystalline wax

Finished size: ¾" square

Beaded frame

Step 1 Thread a needle onto approximately 3' of waxed thread. Leaving a 6" tail, pick up four color-A 11º seed beads, sew through the first bead again, and pull the thread tight to form a ring [fig. 1, a–b]. This is one right-angle weave (RAW) unit.

Step 2 Working in RAW, pick up three color-A beads and sew through the bead that your thread just exited and the next two beads [b–c].

Step 3 Continue in RAW to stitch a total of five units, but for the fifth unit, sew through only one more bead instead of two [c–d].

Step 4 Work four more units as in step 3 [d–e]. Repeat [e–f].

Step 5 Work two units [f–g]. To attach the fourth side to the first side, pick up an 11º, sew through the adjacent bead on the first side [g–h], pick up an 11º, and sew through the end bead on the fourth side. Sew through the next three beads to exit the inside of the square [h–i].

Step 6 Pick up a color-A bead and sew through the next inside edge bead [fig. 2, a–b]. Continue adding color-A beads between each pair of inside beads, all the way around [b–c]. Each square frame should have 12 color-A beads stitched between pairs of edge beads. Sew through the beadwork to exit a middle bead on the inside edge of the original square frame [c–d].

Insert the cube bead

Step 1 Pick up an 8mm cube and sew through the middle bead on the other side of the square frame to anchor the stone cube [photo A].

Step 2 Sew back through the stone cube and through the middle bead on other side of the cube.

The stone cube bead has two thread passes through it at this point. Reinforce the thread path again; these cube beads have sharp edges, and the extra stitches add a bit of extra security.

Step 3 Push the cube into the square frame. Notice how the outer edge of the frame slants down and the inner edge is already building up the side of the stone cube.

Build the bezel

Step 1 With the needle exiting a middle bead on the inside of the frame, sew through the next color-A bead.

Step 2 Working in tubular peyote stitch, pick up a color-A bead, skip a bead, and sew through the next bead in the round.

Step 3 Repeat step 2 all the way around the square frame.

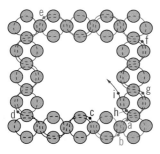

fig. 1

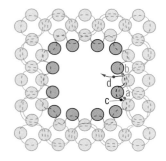

fig. 2

Step 4 At the end of the round, step up, sewing through two beads.

Step 5 Work a round of peyote using color-C 15°s. Pull the thread firmly so that this last round snugs up against the stone cube bead. At the end of the round, step up through two beads and sew through the entire round to tighten all the beads together.

Embellish the frame

Magatamas or drops really set off the shape of the frame and provide extra texture to the piece.

Step 1 The drops will be added in the middle of each side in the first peyote round. Sew through the beadwork to exit a side bead in the first peyote round. Pick up a drop bead, and sew through the next bead in the round. Sew through to the next side. Repeat around the frame. After adding the drops, sew through beadwork so the needle exits a bead on the outer edge of the frame.

Step 2 Pick up a color-B 11° and sew through the next outer edge bead. Continue around, picking up a color-B bead and sewing though each edge bead. Don't skip the corners. The color-B beads will cause the corners to pop out. Pull the thread snug so that the entire piece becomes ever-so-slightly domed and all the beads on the outer edge lock tightly together.

And there you have it: one finished component that can be used many different ways. See the sidebar below for tips on making the elements into a necklace, bracelet, or earrings.

Element options

The Helena necklace is made of 21 elements. I connected 17 for the necklace base with spacer beads between. To achieve a gentle curve along the neckline, I added extra beads along the lower edge. In the center, I added two more vertical elements and one more on each side of that, finishing with briolette drops at the bottom.

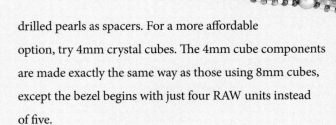

Looking for something with a bit more sparkle? How about using crystal cubes instead of semiprecious stone cubes? If you look at the Helena necklace and compare it to the bracelet shown here, you'll notice quite a difference, achieved simply by changing an organic stone to a brilliant crystal. When designing beadwork, always keep in mind that the overall look of a creation can be changed by bead finishes: matte versus shiny or organic stone vs. sparkling crystal.

For the Helena bracelet, I made 16 elements using 8mm crystal cubes and stitched them together using double-drilled pearls as spacers. For a more affordable option, try 4mm crystal cubes. The 4mm cube components are made exactly the same way as those using 8mm cubes, except the bezel begins with just four RAW units instead of five.

Helena Elements made with 4mm crystal cubes are perfect for earrings like this petite pair. I hung the elements from their points and added pearl dangles.

Stiletto Earrings

stitches
cubic right-angle weave

inspiration
vintage dagger pin

Even a simply stitched project can be stunning when you put beautiful beads together. The stiletto earrings are a simple chain of eight right-angle weave (RAW) stitches, reinforced with a second layer that gives the structure great stability. One surface of each cube is embellished with a crystal or pearl. A crystal drop accented by pearls on each side adds a glowing finish.

This is cubic right-angle weave in its simplest form. Cubic RAW consists of four "walls" stitched into a cube. Each new cube is stitched onto the previous cube. Cubic RAW is a wonderful way to use different shapes of beads and colors in infinite combinations. These earrings feature my favorite combination, walls composed of an 11º seed bead, a 10º hex-cut bead, and an 11º seed bead. The facets of the hex beads impart gorgeous flash to the beadwork.

Experiment to find bead combinations you like. Substitute other beads for the 10º hex beads, such as 8º seed beads, 8º twisted hex beads, or 1.8mm cube beads. Keep the 11º seed beads on each side, but use whatever looks amazing for the center bead.

When the basic framework of your earring is finished, embellish the open areas of each square with beads of your choice, such as 4mm crystal bicones or rounds, side-drilled drops, or 4–5mm pearls or semiprecious stone beads. After the embellishment beads are stitched into the framework, add 15º seed beads between each square to straighten all the sides and fill in the corners.

supplies

2 grams 11º seed beads, semi-matte silver-lined gray

2–3 grams 10º twisted hex-cut beads, nickel plated (metallic dark gray)

1–2 grams 15º seed beads, 462D (a mixture of deep plum, metallic dark blue, and old gold)

8 dark gray freshwater pearls, 4–5mm

12 4 mm crystal bicones, crystal vitrail medium

2 18mm crystal drops, Swarovski art. 8611, crystal cathedral

Pair of earring wires or lever-back earrings

Fireline, 6- or 8-lb. test

Beading needle, #12

Finished length: 2" plus ⅞" drop

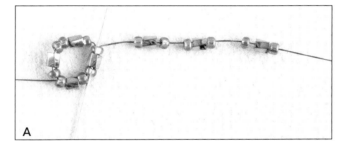

A

Step 1 On 3' of thread, pick up a repeating pattern of an 11º seed bead, a 10º twisted hex bead, and an 11º seed bead four times. Leaving a 12" tail, sew through the first three beads picked up to form a square. Each wall of the square has an 11º, a 10º twisted hex, and an 11º. Pull snug.

Step 2 Pick up a repeating pattern of an 11º, a 10º twisted hex, and an 11º three times. Sew through the three-bead segment of the square your thread exited at the start of this step [photo A]. Continue through and the next two walls, exiting between two 11ºs. Pull thread snug to form another square.

Step 3 Repeat step 2 until you have stitched eight squares. Pull the thread snug to pull the beads into squares. Don't trim the tails. Put this strip aside.

Step 4 Repeat steps 1–3 to stitch an identical strip of eight squares.

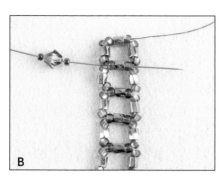

B

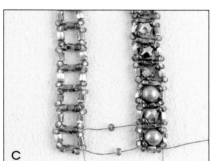

C

Embellish the strip

Step 1 To add embellishment to a RAW strip, sew through the beadwork to exit an 11º at the corner of a segment.

Step 2 Pick up a 15º, a 4mm crystal, and a 15º. Cross over the segment at an angle and sew through the opposite wall [photo B].

Step 3 Continue working down the strip, using pearls in place of the crystals in the sixth and eighth squares.

Sew the pieces together

Step 1 Place one layer over the other, and attach a needle to the tail of the top layer. Sew through the top layer to exit the side wall of the end stitch.

Step 2 Pick up an 11º and sew through the side wall of the corresponding stitch in the other layer.

Step 3 Pick up an 11º and sew through the side wall in the first layer again [photo C]. Following the RAW thread path, sew through the beadwork to exit the next side wall in either layer. Pick up an 11º, and sew through the next side wall in the other layer. Repeat to connect all the corresponding stitches in the two layers. Repeat to connect the other edge.

Colors and finishes for a night on the town

The name "Stiletto Earrings" conjures a color palette of things metallic, dark, and smoky. I started with the nickel-plated 10º twisted hex-cuts. The nickel-plated color of these Miyuki beads is similar to dark pewter and very shiny. Because two shiny AB colors usually compete, my next color choice needed to be decidedly not shiny. I auditioned a matte silver seed bead, but that color combination was dull and not mysterious looking at all. I kept searching and found a semi-matte, silver-lined gray Czech seed. Perfect: The gray beads were glowy but not showy.

My ethereal color choice? A delicious color, Miyuki's DB462 is a mixture of deep plum, metallic blue, and old gold. I used 15º seed beads between each square, and this color contrasts nicely with the gray and silver and plays well with the vitrail bicones.

I've enjoyed exploring many variations of this project. The Thor's Hammer variation above is another interpretation of the technique.

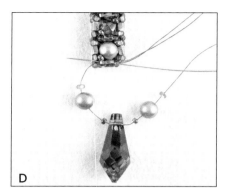

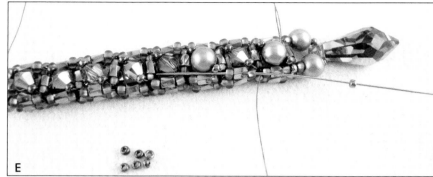

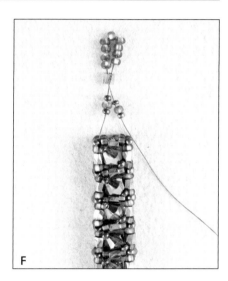

Add the crystal drop

With the needle exiting a bottom corner of an end square, pick up an 11º seed bead, a pearl, a 15º, a crystal drop, a 15º, a pearl, and an 11º . Sew through the end wall again [photo D] and sew through the seed beads, pearls, and crystal drop to reinforce.

Final embellishment

If the thread you are using is getting too short, thread the needle onto another tail. Sew through the beadwork and exit through any three-bead wall along the sides of the earring. Pick up a 15º, and sew through the next three-bead wall along the side of the earring. Repeat all along the side of the earring, adding a 15º at every juncture between the RAW squares [photo E]. Be sure to add 15ºs on the back of the earring as well. Can you see and feel how adding the 15ºs between each segment pulls the beadwork together?

Earring loop

Step 1 Use an untrimmed thread tail to attach the earring loop. Sew through the beadwork to exit an end wall at the top of the earring, and pick up a 15º, an 11º, a 15º, a 10º twisted hex, and nine 11ºs. Sew back through the twisted hex and pick up a 15º, an 11º, and a 15º [photo F], and sew through the end wall again. Sew through to the end wall on the back of the earring.

Step 2 Pick up a 15º, an 11º, and a 15º. Sew through the twisted hex bead from step 1 and on through the nine 11ºs. Sew back through the twisted hex bead. Pull the thread snug so no loops of thread stick out. Pick up a 15º, an 11º, and a 15º. Sew through the end wall on the back of the earring. End the thread. Slip the loop onto an earring wire.

End all threads

At last, time to work in all those thread tails. Clip all of the thread ends close to the beadwork.

Mixed-metal seed beads accented with neutral bicone crystals and smoky quartz briolettes create a warm interpretation (right).

Watch out—you're
wearing stiletto earrings!

Art Deco
Necklace

stitch
cubic right-angle weave

inspiration
Czech glass lentil beads

C zech pressed-glass beads are truly a treasure. Every shape and color imaginable have been created in Czech glass factories and made available in virtually every bead store. So often we see Czech pressed glass beads simply strung; I challenge you to look for novel ways to use them in stitched beadwork.

One day I was hunting through a Czech glass trove in a bead store and I found a hank of tiny glass lentil-shaped beads. The holes were at the top of the beads, and they were coated with a gleaming coppery finish on one side. An interesting bead to look at, but how would I highlight their unusual shape and color in my work? Back in my bead room, playing around making different shapes with cubic right-angle weave (RAW), it occurred to me that I could stitch the two flat pieces together with some other flat, round beads. The tiny lentil beads jumped into the party on my bead tray, and the Art Deco necklace was born.

How do you know if Czech pressed glass will work for stitching two pieces of RAW together? Try sewing two flat components together and check if the Czech glass beads crowd each other. If the beads fit nicely together when stitched, they're good to go!

We learned how to stitch a form of cubic RAW in the Stiletto Earrings project. The Art Deco necklace takes it a little further by stitching two pieces together with a sew-down crystal set into the middle of the beadwork.

supplies

4–5 grams 11º seed beads, gilt-lined opalescent peach, 553 (color A)

10–15 grams 11º hex-cut seed beads in a glorious matte hue that reminds me of the Grand Canyon's wind-carved walls, 514F (color B)

2–3 grams 15º seed beads, 462D (color C)

2 grams 6º seed beads, copper-lined amethyst (color D)

45 4mm freshwater pearls in a bronze peachy color

16 6mm glass lentils

2 10mm sew-down crystals (Swarovski Art. 3200), Crystal Volcano

Beading needle, #12

Fireline or PowerPro, 8-lb. test

Microcrystalline wax

Finished length: 19"

Pendant front

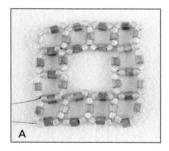
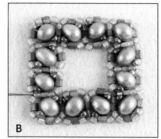

Pendant back

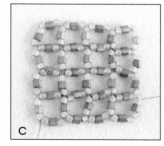
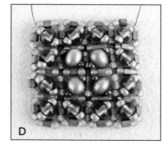

Pendant front

Step 1 Thread a needle onto 3' of waxed thread. Pick up a pattern of a color-A 11º seed bead, a color-B 11º hex bead, and an 11º seed bead four times. Sew through the first three beads picked up, leaving a 6" tail. Pull the thread snug.

Step 2 Pick up a pattern of an A, a B, and an A three times. Sew through the three-bead wall that the needle just exited and the first six beads picked up in this step.

Step 3 Repeat step 2 twice to form a four-square strip, and then sew through the beadwork to exit a side wall of the last square.

Step 4 Repeat steps 2 and 3 twice to create three sides of the frame, and then work a stitch for the fourth side. To connect the fourth side to the first side, pick up an A, a B, and an A, and sew through the side wall at the end of the first strip. Pick up an A, a B, and an A, and sew through the end wall of the previous square [**photo A**].

Step 5 With the needle exiting a three-bead wall of the frame, pick up a color-C 15º, a 4mm freshwater pearl, and a 15º, cross diagonally over the opening in the stitch, and sew through the opposite wall.

Step 6 Repeat step 5 all the way around the frame [**photo B**].

Pendant back

On 3' of thread, repeat steps 1–3 of the pendant front to make a four-square strip. Continuing in RAW, add rows until you have stitched a component that is four rows by four rows [**photo C**].

Some might ask, "Why embellish the back of the necklace?" I say, "Why not?" When I design beadwork, I expect to receive visual and tactile feedback from my creation. Holding a necklace that is embellished on the back draws in the wearer to look on the back; shouldn't they be rewarded? I chose to embellish the back of this necklace with 6º seed beads and pearls in a simple design [**photo D**]. To embellish the back, work as in step 5 of "Pendant front" to fill in every square, substituting 11ºs and 6ºs for the 15ºs and pearls around the perimeter.

Sew the front and back together

Step 1 Place the front and back layers together, and attach a needle to the tail of one layer. Sew through the beadwork to exit an outer-edge side wall.

Step 2 Pick up a lentil bead, and sew through the corresponding outer-edge wall of the other layer.

Step 3 Pick up a lentil, and sew through the wall your thread exited at the start of the previous step [photo E]. Continuing in RAW, work around the outer edge, adding one lentil per stitch.

Add the crystal

Step 1 The sew-down crystal rests in the four-square opening on the front of the pendant. Use a thread on the back of the pendant and sew through the beadwork to exit a center B, making sure the needle points toward the outer edge of the pendant. Sew through one hole of the crystal and pick up a 15º. Sew back through the crystal and the B your thread exited at the start of this step, and continue through to exit the B nearest the other hole in the crystal. Sew through the crystal, pick up a 15º, and sew back through the crystal and the B [photo F]. Sew through the beadwork to exit any three-bead wall in the pendant.

Step 2 To stabilize the pendant and keep all the angles square, add 15ºs at the intersections of the walls: Pick up a 15º, and sew through the next three-bead wall. Repeat at all the intersections on both the front and back of the pendant.

Small beaded components

Step 1 Work in RAW to stitch four segments that are two rows by two rows each. Embellish two of the segments with pearls and the other two with 6º seed beads, as in the pendant.

Step 2 Sew pairs of segments together (one pearl segment and one 6º segment) front to back using 11ºs between the layers instead of lentils. Using the leftover thread tails, add 15ºs at all the intersections, as in the pendant.

Back

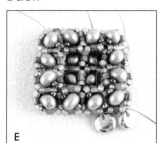

E

Front

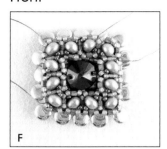

F

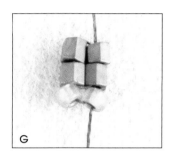

G

Beaded strap

This stitch was used in the Banded Carnelians Necklace. This stitch resembles herringbone stitch, so the beads will line up in columns, two beads wide, with the holes running parallel.

Two beaded straps will attach the pendant to the small components on each side. You'll need to stitch eight chain straps altogether since they are attached in the middle to the beaded components.

Step 1 Thread your needle with 3' of thread. Pick up an A, two Bs, and an A. Sew through the first A and B, leaving a 6" tail. Pull snug.

Step 2 Pick up two Bs, sew down through the next B, and up through the adjacent B and the first new B [photo G].

Step 3 Repeat step 2, picking up two Bs in each stitch, until you have nine rows of Bs. Work one more stitch with As.

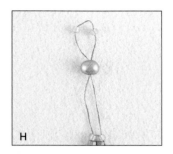

Step 4 Pick up a 4mm pearl and two As, and sew back down through the pearl and the A adjacent to the A your thread just exited [photo H]. Sew through the adjacent A, the pearl, and the first new A.

Step 5 Repeat steps 2–4 three times to stitch a beaded strap that has four repeats of the nine rows of Bs, ending with a pair of As.

Step 6 Repeat steps 1–5 to make a total of eight straps. These work up quickly, so it won't take too long.

Putting everything together

Step 1 Attach two straps to each side of the pendant, which is positioned with a corner pointing up: Connect the two inner straps to the B in the second row on the back of the pendant. The outer straps need to be somewhat longer, so add a 6° seed bead before attaching each strap to the B in the fourth row on the back [photo I]. Repeat on the other side of the center component.

Step 2 Attach the other ends of the straps to a small component: Pick up a 6°, and sew through a B on one edge of the component. Sew back through the 6° and a few beads in one column of the strap. Sew back through the other columns and the B on the other edge of the component.

Step 3 Attach the other strap to the other set of Bs on the edge of the component [photo J].

Step 4 Repeat steps 2 and 3 to attach the remaining straps to the small components.

With this technique, you can create square or rectangular segments for neck straps or to be focal points.

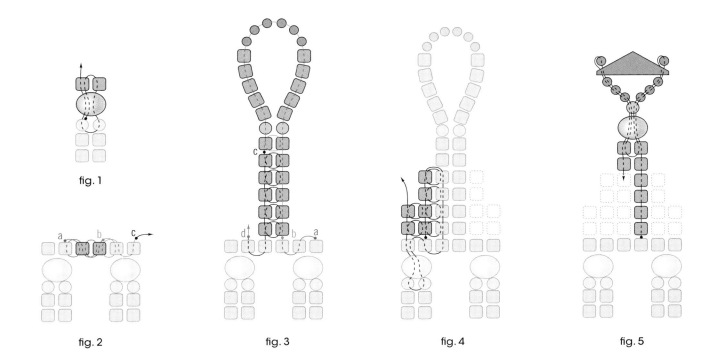

fig. 1

fig. 2

fig. 3

fig. 4

fig. 5

Clasp

Step 1 To make a tab to connect the ends of the straps and make a loop closure, thread a needle on a thread tail exiting an end A on one of the straps.

Step 2 Pick up a 6° and two Bs, and sew back through the 6° and an A. Sew through the adjacent A, the 6°, and the first new B [**fig. 1**].

Step 3 Repeat steps 1 and 2 with the other strap on this end of the necklace.

Step 4 With one of the threads, work two ladder stitches with Bs [**fig. 2, a–b**]. Work a ladder stitch thread path through an end B on the other strap, making sure the strap isn't twisted, and then sew through the next B [**b–c**].

Step 5 Zigzag back through the next two Bs [**fig. 3, a–b**].

Step 6 Pick up six Bs, an A, five Bs, six 15°s, five Bs, an A, and a B. Work a square stitch thread path through the sixth B picked up [**b–c**]. Adding one B per stitch, work five more square stitches, then sew down through the next B and up through the adjacent B [**c–d**].

Step 7 Continuing in square stitch, work a column of four Bs, then a column of two Bs [**fig. 4**]. Sew through the beadwork, and repeat on the other side of the tab.

Step 8 For the other end of the necklace, work as in steps 1–7, but in step 6, pick up six Bs, a 6°, three 15°s, one hole of a crystal, and a 15°. Sew back through the crystal, three 15°s, the 6°, and the next B. Pick up a B, and sew through the 6° again. Attach the other side of the crystal the same way, and then complete the tab [**fig. 5**].

Intergalactic Love
Song Necklace

stitch
cubic right-angle weave

inspiration
art glass focal bead

I am a member of the International Society of Glass Bead Makers, the lone seed beader in this large organization. I began my journey combining beadwork with art glass ten years ago, collaborating with art glass artist Kristen Frantzen Orr to make jewelry that has sold in galleries in the U.S. and Japan. Since then, I have had the luxury of getting to know some of the finest bead makers and fondling their precious beads.

I look at an art glass bead as a half-written story that has been entrusted to me to finish. Andrew Brown never fails to amaze and captivate me with his beads, and the bead I used in this necklace was the inspiration for the entire piece. Looking closely at Andrew's bead, I saw otherworldly rings and spirals of color that resembled pictures sent back from the Hubbell spacecraft. I created a frame for the bead, always being mindful to complement the bead and not overwhelm it.

This necklace looks complicated, but it's simple to stitch in cubic right-angle weave (which I know you've mastered by now!). The results can be stunning. This is the kind of knockout necklace that can take a basic black dress or classic blouse from ho-hum to spectacular.

Art glass beads by Harold Williams Cooney, Jeff Barber, Kristen Frantzen Orr, and Andrew Brown

supplies

- Art glass focal bead or stone bead
- 1 hank or 25–30 grams 11º seed beads, blue-green iridescent
- 55–60 grams 11º two-cut hex beads (can substitute 10ºs), matte gold iris
- 15 grams 15ºs
- 90 4mm glass drops
- 146 4mm bicone crystals
- Fireline, 6 and 8 lb. test
- Beading needles, #10 and #12

Finished length: 19" with 3" focal drop

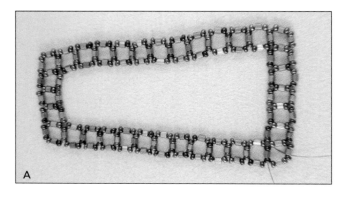

A

Beaded frame for art glass focal

You'll begin by stitching a frame for the focal bead. Since there isn't a standard size for art beads, you may need to customize the frame to fit your focal bead. The frame for this bead is 13 squares high. The top row of the frame is five squares wide and the bottom row is seven squares wide. Each of the right-angle weave (RAW) walls consists of an 11º seed bead, an 11º hex bead, and an 11º. Make the necessary adjustments in the frame design to fit your focal bead.

Step 1 Stitch the first frame in right-angle weave to fit your bead [photo A]. I like to use the 8-lb. Fireline for the frame, starting with a minimum of 3'. Check the fit of the art-glass focal bead in the interior of the frame before completing it; it's better to have the frame slightly larger than the focal bead than smaller. If the focal bead is just ⅛" too big, it will cause the frame to curve and buckle.

Step 2 Stitch a second frame that matches the first frame. Align the frames, and attach a needle on one of the threads. Sew through the beadwork to exit any three-bead wall on an edge. Pick up an 11º, and sew through the corresponding wall in the other frame. Pick up an 11º, and sew through the wall your thread exited at the start of this step. Continuing in RAW, connect the frames along the entire edge, picking up one 11º per stitch. Repeat to attach the inner edges.

Step 3 Add 3' of 6-lb. Fireline in the frame, and exit a center B at the top of the frame. Pick up the focal bead and any additional seed beads if necessary to fit the focal bead perfectly within the frame. (Line the focal bead with flexible tubing, if necessary.) Sew through the center B at the bottom of the frame. Sew back and forth between the top and bottom edges of the frame, connecting to both the front and back layers at least once. Make several passes through the focal bead so it's securely sewn in.

Embellish the beaded frame

Embellishing the surface of the frame is certainly the most fun part of this project, in my opinion. Plan a design with accent beads. I used a combination of 4mm bicone crystals and glass drops. Continue with the 6-lb. Fireline because you'll stitch many thread passes through each foundation bead on the frame. Exit any three-bead wall of the frame, pick up a 4mm crystal or drop bead, cross over the opening in the stitch on a diagonal, and sew through the next wall. Repeat around, sewing either crystals or drops in each square on the front of the frame. I didn't embellish the back of the frame, although you could if you wanted to.

Reinforce the sides

After all the spaces are filled, exit any three-bead wall along an edge. Pick up a 15º, and sew through the next wall. Repeat all along the outer and inner edges on both the front and back of the frame. When all edges of the frame are reinforced with 15ºs, work any short threads into the beadwork and trim. Don't trim longer tails—they will be used for attaching one frame to another.

Make the accent frames

Medium frame: Stitch two medium-sized double-sided frames. I made two frames that are each ten squares high,

74

three squares across at the top, and five squares across at the bottom. Embellish the front of each frame and reinforce the sides, repeating the techniques used for the first frame.

Small frame: Stitch and embellish two smaller frames in the same way. Mine are seven squares high, three squares across at the top, and five squares across at the bottom.

Stitch the frames together

Stitch the frames together along the top row of each frame on both the front and back: Exit an edge wall in the top row of a frame, pick up an 11º, a hex bead, and an 11º, and sew through the edge wall of the next frame. Working in RAW, pick up an 11º, a hex bead, and an 11º, and sew through the wall your thread exited on the previous frame. Attach the back surface the same way, and then sew through to the other edge wall of the top row. Repeat to connect all the frames.

Necklace sides

This necklace is 19" long. If you'd like a shorter or longer necklace, make adjustments as you create the sides of the necklace. Two strips of cubic RAW connect the frames to the clasp. Due to the shape of the rectangular frames and to fit the curve of the neck, I stitched two different lengths. One strip is 22 squares long and the other strip is 28 squares long.

Step 1 Use 3' lengths of the 8-lb. Fireline. Working off the top row of an edge frame, work a strip of RAW that is 22 squares long. Repeat, working the back surface. Join, embellish, and reinforce the two strips as you did the frames.

Step 2 Working off the fourth square on an edge, work two 28-square strips. Join, embellish, and reinforce the two strips as you did the frames. Stitch two strips that are three squares long. Join them as in the frames. This will be a bar section that the sides and the clasp will attach to.

Step 3 Attach the side strips on one end to squares 1 and 3 of the bar section made in step 2.

Step 4 Embellish the surface and reinforce the sides of the bar.

Step 5 Repeat steps 1–4 for the other side of the necklace.

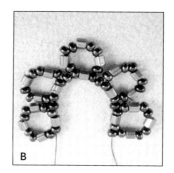

B

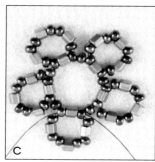

C

Toggle ring

Step 1 On 3' of 8-lb. Fireline, pick up a pattern of an 11º, a hex bead, and an 11º four times. Sew through the first three beads to form a ring, and pick up an 11º. Repeat four times **[photo B]**, then sew through the first three beads in the first ring **[photo C]**. Sew through the next 11º, three-bead inner wall, 11º, and side wall **[fig. 1, a–b]**.

Step 2 Pick up an 11º, a hex, and an 11º, and sew through the adjacent side wall, 11º, the next inner wall, 11º, and the adjacent side wall **[b–c]**.

Step 3 Repeat step 2 twice **[c–d]**.

Step 4 Pick up an 11º, and sew through the next wall **[d–e]**. Repeat, and then sew through the next 11º and wall **[e–f]**.

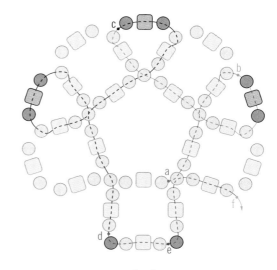

fig. 1

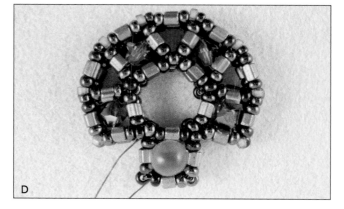

fig. 2

Step 5 Pick up a 15º, and sew through the next wall [fig. 2, a–b].

Step 6 Pick up two 15ºs, and sew through the next wall [b–c].

Step 7 Repeat step 6 five times [c–d].

Step 8 Pick up a 15º, and sew through the next wall [d–e].

Step 9 Repeat steps 1–8 to make another layer, then stitch the layers together as you did the other component.

Step 10 Embellish the five original loops [photo D].

Step 11 Attach the toggle ring to the clasp bar with a RAW stitch, embellish it, and reinforce it.

Toggle bar

The toggle bar for this necklace needs to be fairly firm to support the weight of the beadwork.

Step 1 Thread a needle with 3' of 8-lb. Fireline. Pick up two 11º seed beads, eight hex beads, and two 11ºs [**fig. 3, a–b**]. Work 12 rows of flat, even-count peyote to make a strip with seven beads on each straight edge [**b–c**]. Roll the strip into a tube and zip the ends together.

Step 2 With one end of the remaining thread, sew a drop or a crystal onto the end of the peyote tube. Sew through the crystal or drop several times for strength. Repeat on the other end of the tube.

Step 3 On 2' of 8-lb. Fireline, sew through the top edge of the middle square of the clasp with attached side components.

Step 4 Using Bs, work nine ladder stitches. Sew through a middle bead on the toggle bar. Retrace the thread path several times for security. If desired, embellish the sides with 15ºs: Exiting a B in the ladder, pick up a 15º, and sew through the next ladder B. Repeat along the entire ladder. Repeat in the opposite direction to fill in the gaps. Trim all threads.

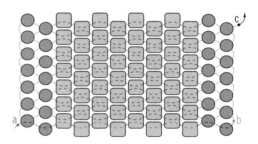

fig. 3

Make dinner reservations because you're going to need a place to show off this necklace!

African Turquoise Tubes Necklace

stitch
brick stitch

inspiration
gemstone tube beads

At bead stores and shows, I can spend hours looking at seed beads—on hanks, in tubes, or neatly displayed in little flip-top cases. A close second to my obsession with seed beads is my love for semiprecious stone beads. But don't fear—this obsession isn't about paying top dollar for expensive briolette and faceted stone beads. Au contraire, many types of stone beads are relatively inexpensive. You'll see them at every show and store, in every size and shape you can wrap your beady mind around.

It's so easy to create a simple strung necklace using stone bead strands. But as a hard-core seed beader, you know you want to do more with that lovely strand of stone beads.

I purchased inexpensive African turquoise tubes knowing that the beautiful bronzy-browns and shades of green and turquoise would fit easily into my favorite color palette. The lovely, elongated stones pose a common challenge: Stringing them is too simple a solution; how can I combine them with stitched beadwork yet not overwhelm them?

I decided to frame the stone beads with brick-stitched bands of seed beads in shades that subtly echo the stone's colors. Brick stitch is often overlooked by beaders in favor of peyote stitch. One of the star qualities of brick stitch is that it can build upon an existing base of thread surrounding a larger bead, which gives you the opportunity to add color and texture to already lovely beads.

Most instructions for brick stitch start off differently than what I'll guide you through. I build a base with two beads at each end of the center bead, and start brick stitching from that base. With this method, I find it easier to achieve symmetry and an identical count of beads on both sides, and the stitches look much neater.

2 16" strands of 30–50mm stone tube beads

10–15 grams metallic bronze 11º hex beads, F4605

10 grams 11º Czech seed beads, turquoise picasso

5 grams 15º seed beads in a mix of five colors:
• silver-lined chartreuse AB, 643A
• pale turquoise matte F374G
• dark gold, 462D
• burnished green-gold, F460R
• amber lined with turquoise, 952

Fireline or PowerPro, 8-lb. test

Loomwork needle or #12 long beading needle

Clasp

Finished length: 21" with 3½" focal drop

My hex beads echo the bronzy colors found in my stone beads and the Picasso-finish turquoise seed beads go well with the deep greens and blues. The 15º seed beads are my chance to place some ethereal colors into this colorway. I have chosen delightful transparent chartreuse, my luscious favorite 462D, the burnished 460R, and amber lined with turquoise. By mixing matte metallic finishes with glitzy AB finishes, I'll have lots of visual interest along the edges of my stone beads without overpowering them. Just more of those sly flashes that catch your eye!

This project uses stone beads that range from 30mm to 50mm, but any length of bead can work. I would suggest not using rectangular beads; a gently tapered oval will work the best. As I started working with the long, tubular stone beads, I discovered that many of my beading needles weren't long enough to pass through the beads. Loomwork needles (often called #12 long) that are about 3" long work well; ask your local bead store if they can get them for you.

The possibilities are endless.
    As I'm fond of saying,
 "If you can dream it,
      you can bead it!"

Frame the stone bead

Step 1 On 3' of thread, pick up a stop bead and sew through it again, leaving a 6" tail. Make sure the stop bead is bigger than the hole in the stone bead; an 8º seed bead will work nicely.

Step 2 Pick up a stone bead and, working in a circular fashion, sew through the stone bead again. You will have a thread bridge on the outside of the stone bead. Repeat three more times to create four thread bridges on the outside of the stone bead.

Step 3 Adjust the thread bridges so you have a pair on each side of the bead. Pull thread snug. The first round of seed beads will attach to these thread bridges.

Step 4 Pick up two 11º hex beads and sew back through the stone bead.

Step 5 Pick up two 11º hex beads and sew back through the stone bead and one of the hex beads from step 4. Sew down through the adjacent hex bead and back through the stone bead and a hex bead at the other end. Remove the stop bead [photo A].

Step 6 Pick up a hex bead, and sew under an adjacent pair of thread bridges. Sew back through the new hex bead and pull snug.

Step 7 Working along the side of the stone bead, pick up a hex bead, sew under the thread bridge, and sew back up through the hex bead. Pull snug.

Step 8 Repeat step 7 until you reach the opposite end of the stone bead.

Step 9 Sew down through a hex bead at this end, and then up through the next hex bead. Now you're ready to start stitching the other side. Repeat steps 6 and 7 to finish the first round of brick stitch. When you finish this edge, sew down through the first hex bead at the other end [photo B], and sew up through the next hex bead.

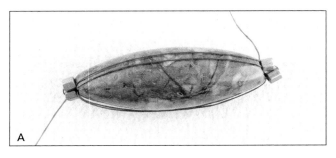

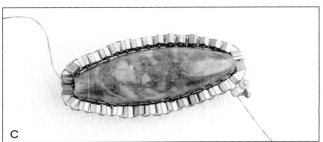

Stitch the second round

Step 1 Pick up an 11º seed bead, a 15º seed bead, and an 11º.

Step 2 Notice the thread bridges that show along the outer edge of the previous round? Sew under the next thread bridge in the previous round, back through the last 11º picked up, and pull snug **[photo C]**. This stitch is often referred to as picot stitch.

Step 3 This next stitch is a little different than the first because you'll pick up two beads instead of three. Pick up a 15º and an 11º Sew under the next thread bridge and back through the last 11º. Pull snug.

Step 4 Repeat step 3 all the way around the edge of the previous round. Make sure that the beads in the picot edging aren't crowded; if the picot starts ruffling, skip a thread bridge and sew under the next one.

Step 5 After the last stitch, pick up a 15º and sew down through the very first 11º from the beginning of the round. Pass through several beads, but don't trim the treads **[photo D]**.

Step 6 Stitch frames for as many stone tubes as desired I stitched 14 framed beads for my necklace, and then played around with the framed stone beads until I found a shape that was interesting. I created a pendant effect by stacking

several beads on top of each other. Can you imagine how stone beads of different lengths would look together?

Put it all together

Connecting the stone tube beads is quite easy because the 15ºs used in the picot stitch interlock when you place two framed beads alongside each other or end to end.

Step 1 Arrange your framed beads in a manner that is pleasing to your eye. Measure the arrangement, making sure it will be long enough for a necklace.

Step 2 Using a thread tail, sew through the beadwork to exit a 15º at a connection point. Sew through a 15º on the next component and then the next 15º on this component. Repeat to attach at least two 15ºs on one component and three 15ºs on another.

Step 3 Repeat step 2 to connect the remaining framed beads.

Step 4 Sew through the beadwork of a component at one end of the necklace, exiting at the point you want the clasp to be attached. Pick up an 8º seed bead, nine 11ºs, and a clasp half. Sew back through the 8º and into the component. Retrace the thread path several times. Repeat at the other end of the necklace.

Easy Big-Sky Earrings

hese earrings are a variation on the African Turquoise Tubes necklace. We'll start by adding a brick-stitch edging around Czech pressed glass tubes or oval pearls. How to choose the center beads to stitch around? For the first pair (which I detail in my instructions), I chose Czech glass beads that were tubular but not angular; sharp angles don't allow the stitches to curve around smoothly. For the variation shown on p. 85, I used two freshwater "rice" pearls—a slightly elongated shape. Choose center beads that have a hole that will accommodate four passes of the needle and thread. Avoid using center beads with rough or sharp openings.

supplies

2 8–12mm oval Czech glass beads, turquoise picasso

1 gram 11º seed beads, 397H gray lined in jonquil (color A)

1 gram 11º Czech seed beads, turquoise picasso (color B)

1 gram size 11º seed beads, matte teal, F154C (color C)

1 gram size 11º seed beads, pale green, 412A (color D)

1 gram 8º seed beads, matte metallic greenish gold, F460R

2 10–12mm drops or briolettes, turquoise

Pair of earring wires

Fireline, 8-lb. test

Beading needle, #10 or #12

Finished length: 2"

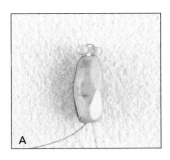
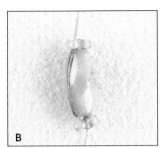
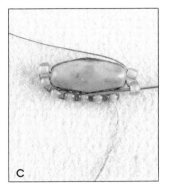

Before you begin stitching, cull all of your seed beads, discarding any that are large or misshapen.

Step 1 Thread a needle onto 3' of Fireline. Sew through an oval bead, leaving a 6" tail. Moving the needle in a circular motion, pass through the oval bead three more times. Pull snug after each pass of the needle.

Step 2 You now have four thread passes around the oval bead. Adjust the thread so you have a pair on each side of the center bead. The seed beads will attach to these thread bridges. Make sure the thread tension is consistent in all four segments.

Step 3 Pick up two color-A 11º seed beads, and sew back through the oval bead [photo A].

Step 4 Pick up two As, and sew back through the oval bead and one of the two As from step 3 [photo B]. The first brick stitch round will be worked off the pairs of beads at the ends of the oval bead.

Begin brick stitching

Step 1 With the thread exiting an A from step 3, pick up an A, and sew under the thread bridges adjacent to the bead the thread is exiting. Sew back through the bead just added, and pull snug.

Step 2 Repeat step 1, working along one side of the oval bead. Make sure the As are snug but not crowded—crowding this round will cause the beadwork to ruffle.

Step 3 At the end of the round, sew down through the first bead of the remaining pair [photo C], and up through the next bead. Resume stitching around the other side of the oval bead as in steps 1 and 2.

Step 4 At the end of the round, sew down through the first bead at the other end [photo D]. This is the foundation round.

Next row: Add the 8ºs

Because this design is built on an oval or round form, each additional round of brick stitch needs to increase slightly in size. We'll use 8ºs in the next round. Notice how there are thread bridges showing on the outer edge of the previous brick-stitched round. The next round will be attached to those thread bridges.

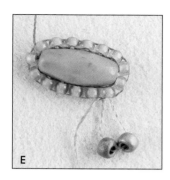

E

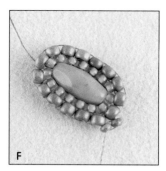

F

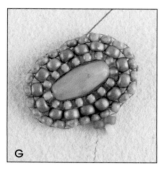

G

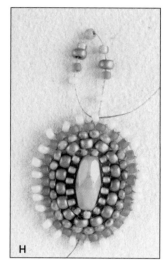

H

I

between the 11⁹s, so this next round will require two 11⁹s stitched onto each thread bridge.

Step 1 With the thread exiting the top of an 8⁹ from the previous round, pick up two color-B 11⁹s and sew under the nearest thread bridge and back up through the second B [photo F].

Step 2 Work in brick stitch, placing two Bs above each thread bridge. If you see crowding or ruffling, stitch just one B above a thread bridge and resume placing two per thread bridge on the next bridge. Finish stitching around the perimeter and connect the last bead to the first bead as in previous rounds.

Step 3 The last round is different; you'll add two bead colors in each stitch. With the needle exiting a B in the outer edge, pick up a color-C 11⁹, a color-D 11⁹, and a C. Sew under the next thread bridge in the previous round, sew back through the last C, and pull snug so the D pops out to the very outer edge [photo G].

Step 4 Pick up a D and a C. In brick stitch, sew under the next thread bridge and back through the C. See how this stitch creates a picot type of edging?

Step 5 Repeat step 4 around the perimeter of the beadwork. Connect to the first C at the end of the round, adding a D between the first and last Cs. Sew through several beads to secure the stitch. Do not trim.

Earring wire loop

Remember that 6" tail I asked you to leave at the beginning of this project? It will come in very handy for attaching an earring loop.

Step 1 Sew up through the rows of beads to exit a D that is centered over the center oval bead.

Step 2 Pick up a D, a C, an 8⁹, an A, a B, an A, an 8⁹, a C, and a D. In a circular motion, sew through the D your thread exited at the start of this step [photo H]. Circle through several times for strength, and then sew down through the work. Tie a half-hitch knot onto an existing thread, bury the thread in a bead, and trim.

Step 1 With the needle exiting outward, pick up two 8⁹s and sew under the next thread bridge [photo E]. Please note that the first stitch of this and future rounds requires two beads instead of one. Sew back up through the second 8⁹.

Step 2 Continue in brick stitch around the perimeter, stitching one 8⁹ onto each thread bridge. When you reach the end of the round, sew down through the first 8⁹ to attach and complete this round.

Now it gets interesting

The previous round increased by substituting 8⁹s for 11⁹s. The thread bridges between the 8⁹s are longer than those

Add the dangle

Step 1 Place a needle on the remaining thread, and sew through the beadwork to exit a D opposite the hanging loop.

Step 2 Pick up a D, a C, an 8º, an A, a drop bead, an A, an 8º, a C, and a D. In a circular motion, sew through the D your thread just exited. Check to see how the drop bead hangs. If it looks good, sew through all the beads just added a few times to reinforce. Sew back up through the beadwork. Tie a half-hitch knot somewhere along the way, bury the thread, and trim. Open the loop of an earring wire, and attach the hanging loop.

I bet you can't wait to make the second one!

Parasol earrings variation

I do love shades of green and turquoise! My mother used to wear many Navajo bracelets stacked up her arms. When I was young, while sitting near her, I would rub the turquoise stones, feeling that special texture that only turquoise has. They were as blue as the Arizona sky. But every so often, we all need to be pulled out of our comfortable box of the familiar—including me. In designing this project, that could mean only one thing: I had to make a pair of pink earrings.

These earrings are made the same way as the Big Sky Earrings, but with these materials and color substitutions:

- Mauve rice pearl for the center bead
- Matte gold 11º seed beads (color A)
- Coppery pink matte 11º seed beads, F4605 (color B)
- Bright, brassy 11º seed beads, 457 (color C)
- 3mm Swarovski art. 5000 in Sand Opal—my ethereal color (replacing the 8º seed bead)
- Gilt-lined peach-color 15ºs, 553 (color D)

The drop and earring loop feature 3mm pearls in lilac, and the drop is a faceted pink chalcedony briolette. Now you have two earrings made exactly the same way but with a totally different effect just by changing the colors. Where the turquoise colorway was dramatic, the pink earrings are delicate. I call them my Parasol Earrings.

Here are a few tips that I learned along the way when stitching up the Parasol Earrings: The crystal beads are translucent, so Crystal Fireline is the perfect thread to use. (I tried Fireline in Smoke and dark green PowerPro; both muddied the color of the crystals.) The light thread disappeared inside the crystal, much to my delight. Along the outer edges of the earring, I started really appreciating the rosy pink of the matte seed beads and the tiny 15ºs. To further intensify the effect of these colors, I used a permanent marker to color the thread hot pink. (It scared me, but I did it anyway!) The effect was subtle, yet it definitely added another layer of color. I also modified the dangle and the earring loop just a bit.

Urban Bedouin Cuff

stitches
loomwork or square stitch,
picot edging/bead embroidery

inspiration
vintage Bedouin bracelet

I am enamored of the old, ethnic look of Bedouin jewelry. As I sketched various ideas for using it as inspiration, I realized it would be too much of a cliché to interpret in a literal way by sewing Bali silver beads onto silver seed beads. Instead, I chose to take the design elements of the Bedouin cuffs I love and interpret them in a contemporary way.

As the saying goes, "Everything is in the details," and often I apply this aphorism to jewelry construction. While the beading techniques are quite easy for this project, there are many steps in the construction of the bracelet. The lesson you will discover if you choose to make this project is this: If you are willing to put in hours of beading a project, please invest that same level of care in the construction and finishing steps.

supplies

20 grams 11º three-cut Czech seed beads, gray AB, culled for size and shape

15–20 grams 15º seed beads, dark silver color, shiny finish

4x9" piece of thin silver leather (glove leather or kidskin)

3x9" piece of leather or Ultrasuede for lining

18 4x8mm rondelle pearls, dark silver color, flat on one side

2" wide brass cuff blank

Beading needle, #10

Bead embroidery needle (also known as a sharp)

Adhesive sheets (Therm O Web)

Fireline, 6 lb. or 8 lb. test

Small, sharp scissors

Small smooth-jawed pliers

Beading loom (optional)

A

My gorgeous, glittering, gray three-cut beads

The Czech seed beads I chose for this project have a lovely glittering finish due to their facets. I chose to leave the smooth fabric of loomed beads unembellished; the soft gray was enough sparkle without going over the top. If I were to make this bracelet using an opaque, plainer color of seed beads, I would certainly consider sewing down some beaded embellishment on the strip.

Stitch the strip

Step 1 Use a loom or square stitch to stitch a strip 14 beads wide and 80 rows long with the 11º three-cuts. Don't trim any long thread tails; they can be used later in the project. (If you're looming this strip, trim the warp threads to 2" and adhere them to the underside using Therm O Web.)

Step 2 Using the 15º seed beads, stitch a simple picot edging: Exiting an edge bead in the very last row, pick up three 15ºs and sew down through the next 11º on the edge and up through the following 11º Pull the thread so the three 15ºs sit correctly and the thread disappears between rows.

Step 3 Repeat step 2 along the edge to the end of the strip. After adding the final three 15ºs, sew through the last row of the beaded strip to the other side.

Step 4 Repeat steps 2 and 3 on this side. Pass through a few rows of the beaded strip to secure the thread, but don't trim the tail [photo A].

Make the cuff template

A sheet of printer paper or tissue paper makes easy work of tracing an accurate template for a metal cuff blank that's already curved and shaped. Place the face of the blank onto the paper and gently crease the paper all around the edges. This will leave a creased outline that will be an accurate measurement for cutting the leather strip. Trace along the creased lines with a marker and then cut out along the lines. Use this paper template to trace the outline and its center point on the wrong side of the leather. Mark another line ¾" to 1" outside of the template outline. Cut the leather following the outside line.

On the paper template, arrange the rondelle pearls in a pleasing pattern. My silvery gray rondelle pearls remind me of studs because they are somewhat flat on one side. I spaced the rondelles out (⅝" apart) so that the leather really had room to show; you may prefer your pearls closer together. Mark the placement for the pearls on the wrong side of the leather, moving from the center toward the ends.

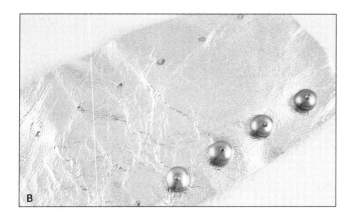

B

Stitch the pearls

Step 1 Thread a needle with approximately 2' of Fireline. (I suggest using a sharps needle for this bead embroidery step.) Beginning at one of the marks on the back of the leather, make two tiny stitches to lock in the thread. Sew back through on the mark to the right side of the leather.

Step 2 Pick up a pearl and a 15º seed bead. Sew back through the pearl and the leather. Pull gently but firmly to tighten the pearl. Sew up through the next mark on the back of the leather. Maintain even thread tension when attaching the pearls [photo B]. Too loose and the pearls will dangle; too tight and the leather will pucker.

Step 3 Repeat step 2 to attach all the pearls.

Attach the beaded strip to the leather

Step 1 Cut a ½x3" strip of adhesive and affix it to the back side of the beaded strip, directly to the beads but avoiding the edge of the beadwork. Using the narrow strip of adhesive will help keep the strip in place while you stitch it onto the leather.

Step 2 Center the beaded strip, adhesive side down, on the right side of the leather, checking placement with the center point markings on the back of the leather. Position the strip lightly, check again for placement, and press the beaded strip gently onto the leather.

Step 3 Using 2' of Fireline, make two tiny stitches under the strip to lock the thread in place. Pass through the leather and directly under an 11º along one edge of the beaded strip.

Step 4 Sew through the 11º and then down through the leather to the back. Skip three beads' width and sew up through the leather, directly under another edge bead. Sew through the 11º and back down through the leather.

Step 5 Repeat step 4 to stitch around the entire strip, securing it to the leather.

Sew the embellished strip to the cuff blank

I like to mark guide points on the brass cuff blank using a permanent marker, on both sides. Remember that you'll place a lining inside the cuff; having center marks will help with correct placement.

Step 1 Cut a strip of adhesive slightly smaller than the cuff blank and apply it to the outside of the blank. (You can also use E6000 or other liquid adhesive for this step.)

Step 2 Carefully place the embellished leather strip onto the blank using the center marks as guides. Resist the urge to smooth the leather down until you have the perfect placement!

Step 3 Cut another strip of adhesive and apply to the inside of the cuff blank. (The paper template you made at the beginning of the project is really handy for cutting out the adhesive strips.) Cut ¼" inside the template line.

Step 4 Place the uncut lining on the inside of the cuff blank, starting in the middle at the center marks. Gently smooth the leather out to the edges.

Step 5 Take a moment and look at the unfinished cuff. An embellished leather strip is affixed to the outside, and your lining is adhered to the inside. It's time to trim both pieces of

Tip MAKE THE LINING BIGGER. I recommend starting with a piece of lining that's slightly larger than the cuff blank—perhaps about 3x8". This will make up for any difficulty you have in aligning everything perfectly (the adhesive on the inside of the cuff blank makes this especially challenging). After the leather is glued down, you can trim the lining to the correct size.

Lining Without Limits

The lining of a bead embroidery project is a great place to show some flair, whether we're talking a pendant, a neckpiece, or a cuff bracelet. Although linings and backs are somewhat hidden, wouldn't it be cool to use an outrageous leather such as hot pink, bright turquoise, or a zebra stripe pattern? Keep an open mind when shopping for leather; you never know what treasures you might find.

C

Design Evolution

For the first Urban Bedouin Cuff I stitched, I used a three-bead picot at the top of each pearl instead of the one-bead embellishment I describe here. I loved the look of it, but I'm always concerned about wearability and longevity of my beadwork. I realized the extra height of the picot would create a point of wear, and so I opted for the practicality of the single-bead embellishment.

leather—carefully. Use sharp scissors that will slice through the leather neatly. Trim both pieces of leather one at a time, to the same size leaving approximately ⅛" allowance beyond the edge of the cuff blank.

Edging

For the finishing touch on this piece, I wanted to interpret the silver edge of my Bedouin inspiration piece in seed beads. I used a "binding stitch," basically a whip stitch plus beads.

Step 1 Thread 3' of Fireline onto a sharps needle. I tend to use a longer piece of thread for edging because I don't like to run out of thread at this point. Your small pair of smooth-jawed pliers will be helpful at this stage for pulling the needle through the two layers of leather.

Step 2 Along the edge, make several small stitches through the lining to lock the thread into place, leaving a short tail. Sew through the lining to exit toward the back of the cuff.

Step 3 Pick up three 15⁰s, and sew down through the top layer of leather and the lining layer, exiting about a bead's width from the previous stitch. Repeat around the perimeter of the cuff. Keep the spacing consistent; don't crowd the stitches, but avoid gaps [photo C]. This stitch covers the raw edges of the leather and looks really good too!

When you've stitched all the way around the cuff, bury the thread in several of the 15⁰s. Carefully trim all threads.

Let's finish this beauty!
You've got a lunch date with friends.

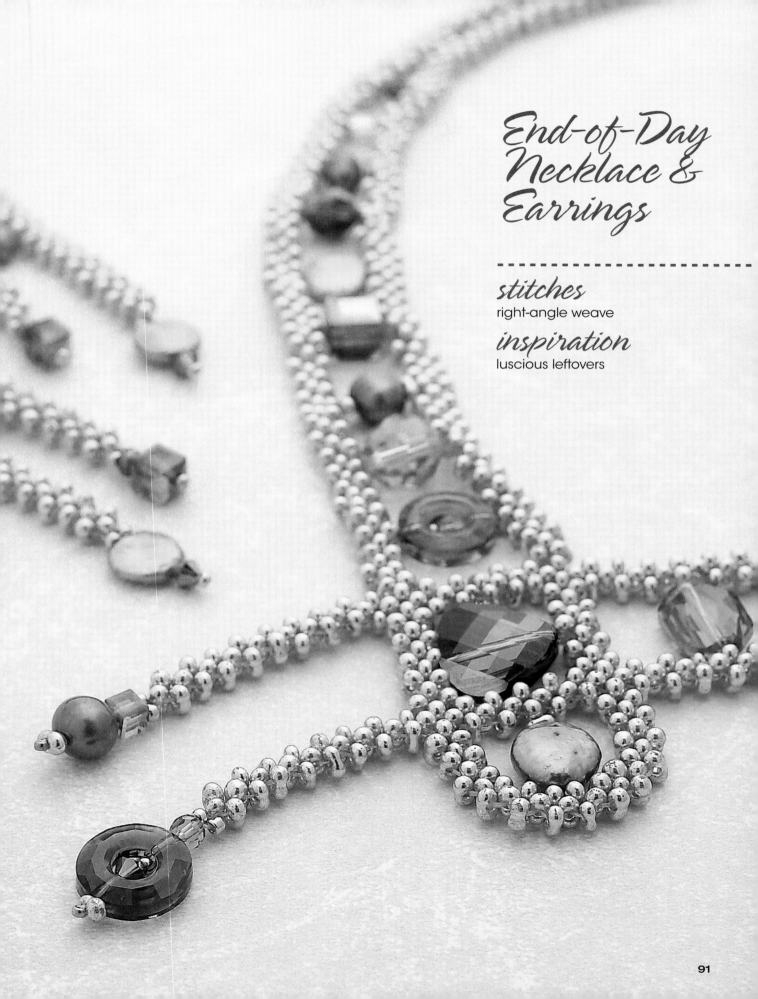

End-of-Day Necklace & Earrings

----

stitches
right-angle weave

inspiration
luscious leftovers

*T*his project takes its inspiration from luscious leftovers… you know, the onesies and twosies of crystals and pearls found in any beader's stash. They remind me of the leftovers of brilliant chips in the glassblower's studio, combined in an impressionist's palette into a "end-of-day" glass vessel.

I often look to vintage rhinestone jewelry for inspiration. The shapes, forms, and silhouettes are sublime, but what about the flashy sparkle-overload of crystals and rhinestone? Shiny, in-your-face styling normally doesn't appeal to my fashion sense. This necklace and earrings set uses crystals and pearls in all shapes and sizes, but bright gold farfalle beads unify the piece and keep the assortment of crystals from looking like a crazy quilt. Isn't it true that when we push ourselves to try new stitches, different colors, and fresh styles, we grow as creative beings?

The fantastic farfalle beads are also called berry, peanut, or bowtie beads. Once you have used these beauties, there's no going back! They interlock when stitched, resulting in stable, substantial beadwork. Right-angle weave normally has a tendency to shift around, but with farfalle, the beadwork is as stable as it is lovely. The double thickness of the farfalle gives the beadwork a hefty feel that I love.

I chose to make my earrings match each other, but if you have a splendid assortment of different crystals and pearls, feel free to echo the free-form nature of the necklace and make unmatched earrings. Adjust the lengths of the dangles to suit your taste.

necklace supplies

20 grams 2x4mm farfalle beads, gold

10 grams 11º seed beads, gold

4–10 grams 15º seed beads, gold

Assortment of crystals and pearls in graduated sizes, 4–12mm

3-loop clasp

Fireline, 6 or 8 lb. test, crystal

Finished length: 17"

Supply note: Czech farfalle are ever-so-slightly smaller than Japanese-made farfalle. Either will work; just don't mix them in the same project.

A nicely draped necklace that fits the contours of a neckline is a joy to wear. A mannequin or dressmaker's bust is a valuable tool. I can pin beaded sections to the bust, step back, and take a look at what I've stitched. Checking for proper length and fit is much easier when the beadwork is on something shaped like the human body.

Step 1 Thread a needle with a comfortably long thread. Pick up four 2x4 farfalle beads, and sew them in a ring. Using farfalle beads, work two more right-angle weave (RAW) stitches. Work five more rows three stitches across to finish the end tab that will connect to the clasp.

Step 2 Exiting the last stitch as though you were going to work another row, work a 53-stitch strip of RAW. Don't trim the thread.

Step 3 Thread a needle with a comfortable length of thread. Weave this new thread into the end tab, and exit the first stitch in the last row of the tab as though you were going to start a new row. Stitch another long strip of RAW, this one 57 stitches long. Don't trim the thread.

Step 4 Repeat steps 1–3 for the left side of the necklace, but make one strip 46 stitches long and the other strip 70 stitches long. This longer strip will create the curve at the bottom right of the necklace. The dangles will be added after you create the overall shape.

Stitch crystals and pearls between strips

Step 1 Arrange the strips so the two shorter strips are on the inside.

Step 2 Arrange an assortment of beads and crystals to fit between both sets of strips. Arrange them so the smaller beads are at the ends and the larger beads are toward the center. Reserve the largest accent bead for the central area where the strips cross. Plan to incorporate a few small beads at the ends of the strips.

Step 3 Thread a needle onto a comfortable length of thread. Sew this thread into the existing beadwork near the point where an outer strip of RAW diverges from the end tab. Following the existing thread path, sew down to exit the inside edge bead of the 14th RAW stitch.

Step 4 Pick up a 4mm crystal (bicone or round). Sew through the inside edge bead of the 13th stitch on the inner RAW strand. Sew back through the crystal and the edge bead, entering this edge bead from the opposite side. This will center the crystal onto the RAW edge stitch.

Step 5 Sew through the next four stitches in the strip, and add the next accent between the strips as in step 4. Continue to add the accent beads in this manner, adjusting the spacing on the straps as needed to achieve the desired drape. For my necklace, I left three RAW stitches between most accent beads. As the necklace curves, there are four RAW stitches between accent beads on the outer RAW strip between accent beads 5 and 7. Tailor the placement to suit the selection of accent beads you use.

Step 6 Add accent beads to the other side of the necklace in the same way.

Create the focal piece

Step 1 Attach a needle to the thread exiting the short strip on the left side of the necklace. Pick up a farfalle bead, sew through the appropriate edge bead of the inner strip on the other side of the necklace. Pick up a farfalle bead, and sew through the bead your thread exited at the start of this step, the first new bead, and the following bead **[figure, a–b]**.

Step 2 Sew through to the other edge of the strip **[b–c]**, work four stitches, and attach the strip to the outer strip on the other side of the necklace **[c–d]**.

Step 3 Attach a needle to the short strip on the right side of the necklace. Attach it to the outer strip on the left side of the necklace as in steps 1 and 2 **[e–f]**. Work eight stitches, and add assorted accent beads at the end **[f–g]**.

Step 4 Attach the outer strip on the right side of the necklace to the outer strip on the left side of the necklace **[h–i]**. Work eight stitches, and add assorted accent beads at the end **[i–j]**.

Step 5 Curve the long strip from the left side around to match up with the stitch that the short strip is attached to. Attach it as in step 1 **[k–l]**.

Step 6 Now that the strips are all connected, fill the center and end spaces with accent beads.

Add the clasp

With the thread tail at one end of the necklace, sew through a clasp loop and back into the end tab. Repeat to attach each loop of the clasp, retracing the thread path several times for extra strength. Repeat on the other end of the necklace, making sure that the other side of the clasp isn't upside down. It may help to close the clasp before attaching **[photo A]**. Weave tails back into the beadwork following the thread path. Trim the threads.

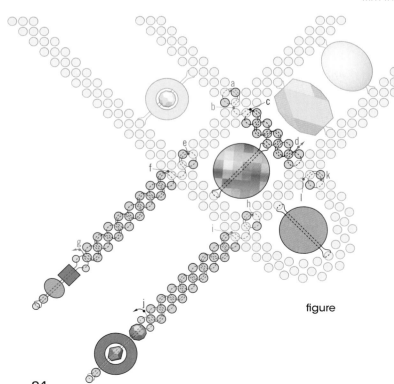

figure

earrings supplies

10 grams 2x4mm farfalle seed beads, gold

20 11º seed beads, shiny gold to match the farfalle beads

10–14 assorted 3–8mm accent beads (crystals, pearls, and cubes)

Pair of matching gold earring posts

Fireline, 8 lb. test, crystal

Beading needle, #10

Finished length: 3"

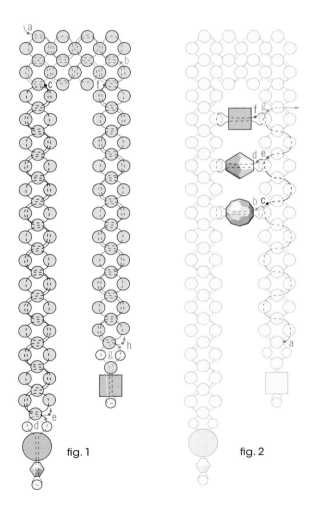

fig. 1   fig. 2

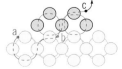

fig. 3

Stitch the earring base

Step 1 Thread a needle with 2' of Fireline. Working in right-angle weave (RAW), pick up four farfalle beads and sew through all the beads twice to secure the thread. Leave a generous 10" tail. Work three more stitches [**fig. 1, a–b**], and then work another row of four stitches [**b–c**]. Working from the bottom of the last stitch, work a vertical row of 14 stitches [**c–d**].

Step 2 Pick up an 11º seed bead, one or more accent beads, and an 11º. Sew back through the accent bead(s), pick up an 11º, and sew through the bottom farfalle bead [**d–e**]. Pull thread snug to firmly seat the dangle beads, and then sew up through the beadwork to exit the earring at **point f.**

Step 3 Work 11 vertical stitches [**f–g**].

Step 4 Pick up an 11º, one or more accent beads, and an 11º. Sew back through the accent bead(s). Pick up an 11º, and sew through the bottom farfalle bead [**g–h**]. Sew up through the previous six stitches [**fig. 2, a–b**].

Step 5 Pick up an accent bead, and sew through the corresponding farfalle bead on the other side of the dangle. Sew back through the accent bead and the farfalle bead on the first side [**b–c**]. Sew through the next two stitches [**c–d**].

Step 6 Pick up an accent bead, and sew through the corresponding farfalle bead on the other side. Sew back through the accent bead and the farfalle bead on the first side [**d–e**]. Sew through the next two stitches [**e–f**].

Step 7 Pick up an accent bead, and sew through the corresponding farfalle bead on the other side. Sew back through the accent bead and the farfalle bead on the first side [**f–g**].

Step 8 Thread a needle onto the thread tail, and sew through the top row to exit the top of the second stitch [**fig. 3, a–b**]. Work two RAW stitches [**b–c**].

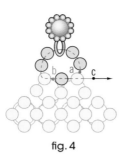

fig. 4

Step 9 Pick up two 11ºs, the loop/jump ring on the post earring, and two 11ºs, and sew through the adjacent farfalle bead, stitching in a circular direction **[fig. 4, a–b]**. Pick up an 11º, and sew through the next farfalle bead **[b–c]**. Retrace the thread path through the connection, and bury the end of the thread in the body of the earring.

Step 10 Make another earring to match … or not.

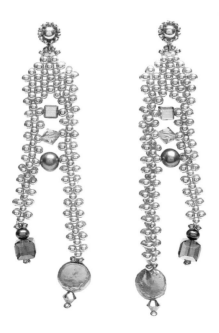

Aren't these fun? I challenged myself by using shiny gold seed beads, which are definitely not something that I use regularly. I was able to use crystals and pearls that were remnants and leftovers from previous projects. I learned that sparkly is not that bad!

Vintage Jewelry = Good Design

For many of us, seeing vintage rhinestone pieces is where we first fell in love with jewelry. I have fond memories of looking through my mother's jewelry box. The treasures I found in there weren't valuable in a monetary sense. They were treasures to me because there was a story behind each one, like the old Navajo bracelets, a tiny locket, or a single earring forever missing its mate. Mama had a rhinestone necklace that always captivated my imagination. I would look into the sparkling rhinestones, fascinated by the brilliant flashes reflected onto the wall.

If you look through collections of rhinestone jewelry, either in books or in antique stores, it's easy to see that there's much more than just sparkle to these pieces. These pieces are perfect examples of good design, form, and silhouette. The graduated strands lie perfectly, not crowded or jumbled. The "chained rhinestone" necklaces feature draping and swagging that follow the contours of the body. Good design, indeed.

Fast-forward to the present day. The jewelry that I create shows how I want to present myself and typify my style. I'm not totally in the sparkly tribe, preferring ethnic jewelry or beadwork featuring organic colors and textures. That said, I am always on the lookout for good forms to follow, and vintage jewelry has that in abundance.

On the following page is an easy exercise for creating jewelry inspired by the silhouettes of vintage jewelry.

Create a template for vintage-inspired jewelry

Find a picture of vintage rhinestone jewelry that you want to translate into beadwork. Using tracing paper, trace the contours or lines of the vintage piece. Write down any ideas or color combinations that come to you while you're tracing.

If you weren't able to enlarge the original picture, use a scanner or photocopier to enlarge the tracing to wearable size. Make several copies so you can cut out one copy and place it around your neck to check the fit. After you adjust the size, the tracing becomes a template: You can start designing your necklace.

Think about different characteristics of beading stitches. Tubular herringbone stitch will curve and drape much better than tubular peyote. Right-angle weave would work quite well and can be embellished easily.

What about bead types? Keep in mind that jewelry that contours and drapes will need to flex and shape to the body. Cube beads and hex-shaped beads naturally tend to become straight, angular shapes as they are stitched together. Cylinder beads fit together like stacked bricks. Czech and Japanese seed beads are much rounder—perfect for stitches that curve.

Are you inspired to go on your own treasure hunt at an antique fair or in vintage jewelry books? I think I'll take out my mother's rhinestone necklace and just look at it for a while.

Sweet Fire, *2007.*
Art glass focal bead by
Kristen Frantzen Orr.
Czech two-cut seed beads,
Japanese seed beads, fresh-
water pearls, carnelians,
crystals, and gemstone
briolettes. Diagonal peyote
stitch. David Orr photo.

Tidepools Reflecting Prometheus, 2009.
Art glass disc beads by Kristen Frantzen Orr.
Czech and Japanese seed beads, freshwater
pearls, tourmaline rondelles, leather backing.
Seed bead embroidery, peyote stitch.
David Orr photo.

Watch Where You Step on the Forest Floor, *2006. Art glass focal bead by Kristen Frantzen Orr. Japanese seed beads and cube beads, crystals, freshwater pearls. Square stitch, stringing, peyote stitch. David Orr photo.*

Cote d'Azure, 2007. Art glass focal bead and accent beads by Kristen Frantzen Orr. Czech and Japanese seed beads, turquoise, freshwater pearls, sugilite, brass buttons. Stringing. David Orr photo.

Belo Horizonte Cuff, 2003. Art glass focal bead by Kristen Frantzen Orr. Czech and Japanese seed beads, wire armature. Herringbone stitch. David Orr photo.

RAW Architecture, 2010. Red Creek Jasper focal and accent beads, Japanese seed beads, freshwater pearls, crystals. Right-angle weave and tubular herringbone stitch. Larry Sanders photo.

Pardon me … there's a bug on your shoulder, 2011. Epaulette—Czech and Japanese seed beads, Swarovski crystals, freshwater pearls, pin-back fastener, leather backing. Beetle—Japanese dichroic glass-coated seed beads, Japanese cylinder beads, wire on a felt armature. Deone Jahnke photo.

When Elements Conspire, 2009. Art glass focal bead by Kristen Franzten Orr. Czech two-cuts, turquoise Picasso seed beads, Japanese seed beads, freshwater pearls, crystals, turquoise. Right-angle weave, peyote stitch, tubular herringbone stitch. David Orr photo.

Artifact Necklace, 2008.
Art glass focal bead by
Kristen Frantzen Orr.
Japanese hex beads,
freshwater pearls,
turquoise. Diagonal
peyote stitch.
David Orr photo.

Techniques Review

ADDING AND ENDING THREAD

Here's the scenario: You're beading away and you've found that sweet spot in the stitches, zooming along on a cuff bracelet that you can't wait to wear. The inevitable happens: You run out of thread and need to start a new thread.

Adding new thread can be problematic. The new thread needs to be secure and not prone to pulling out. The last thing you want is to be able to see where you added the new thread.

My example is a section of tubular herringbone beadwork, which eats up thread quickly.

When the working thread is about 4" long, take a minute and start a new thread. It's wise to add thread when the working thread is still long enough to weave back into the beadwork.

Never—I repeat, never—weave the working thread back into the work before adding a new thread. Why such harshness? When you weave in the working thread, it becomes difficult to know where you left off. This is especially true when using peyote stitch. So, don't work in that too-short thread yet!

Step 1 With the working thread, sew under the thread between two beads in a previous stitch. Pull the thread to create a loop [photo A]. Sew through the loop [photo B] and pull snug. This, in effect, ties the thread onto the last stitch. This is called a half-hitch knot. Sew through a few more beads, following the thread path of the stitch.

Step 2 Thread the needle onto a new length of thread. Place a double overhand knot about 4" from the end of the new thread.

Step 3 Starting five or six rows back in the beadwork, sew through two beads in the row where the old thread ends [photo C]. Pull the thread until the knot is lodged in a bead.

Step 4 Now make a half-hitch knot with the new thread and sew through another bead.

Next I like to put in a square stitch. Sew through an adjacent bead and the bead your thread just exited. This really locks in the new thread so there's no chance of it pulling out. Call it overkill, but between the overhand knot, the half-hitch knot, and the square stitch, the new thread is locked firmly into place. Sew through the beadwork to exit where the old thread was left dangling.

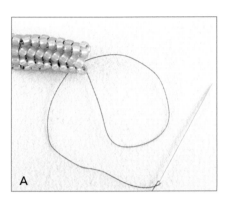

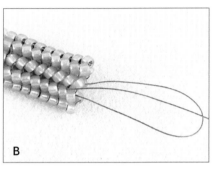

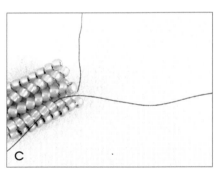

Step 5 Continue stitching with the new thread. When you have stitched a few rows with the new thread, go back and weave in the old thread and the tail of the new thread, making half-hitch knots along the way.

ADDING THREAD TO OTHER TYPES OF STITCHES

Does your beadwork have a right and wrong side? If so, try adding the new thread on the back of the beadwork. The additional thread will not be so visible if it's added on the back.

"Follow the Way of the Thread Path": No, I'm not turning into a Shaolin master, but this bit of wisdom is a good mantra to follow. When adding a new thread, be mindful of the thread path in the existing beadwork (especially important with right-angle weave). Follow that thread path!

CONDITIONING THREAD

Use beeswax or microcrystalline wax (not candle wax or paraffin) or Thread Heaven to condition nylon beading thread and Fireline. Wax smooths nylon fibers and adds tackiness that will stiffen your beadwork slightly. Thread Heaven adds a static charge that causes the thread to repel itself, so don't use it with doubled thread. Both conditioners help thread resist wear. To condition, stretch nylon thread to remove the curl (Fireline doesn't stretch). Pull the thread through the conditioner.

BEADED BACKSTITCH

To stitch a line of beads, come up through the fabric from the wrong side. Pick up three beads. Place the thread where the beads will go, and sew through the fabric right after the third bead. Come up between the second and third beads, and go through the third bead again. Pick up three more beads, and repeat. For a tighter stitch, pick up only one or two beads at a time.

LADDER STITCH

Traditional method

Step 1 Pick up two beads, sew through the first bead again, and then sew through the second bead [a–b].

Step 2 Add subsequent beads by picking up one bead, sewing through the previous bead, and then sewing through the new bead [b–c]. Continue for the desired length. This technique produces uneven tension, which you can easily correct by zigzagging back through the beads in the opposite direction.

Crossweave method

Step 1 Center a bead on a length of thread with a needle attached to each end.

Step 2 Working in crossweave technique, pick up a bead with one needle, and cross the other needle through it [a–b and c–d]. Add all subsequent beads in the same manner.

Forming a ring: If you are going to work in tubular brick or herringbone stitch, form your ladder into a ring to provide a base for the new technique. With your thread exiting the last bead in the ladder, sew through the first bead and then through the last bead again.

TUBULAR HERRINGBONE STITCH

Step 1 Work a row of ladder stitch to the desired length using an even number of beads. Form it into a ring to create the first round. Your thread should exit the top of a bead.

Step 2 Pick up two beads, sew down through the next bead in the previous round [a–b], and sew up through the following bead. Repeat to complete the round [b–c].

3 You will need to step up to start the next round. Sew up through two beads the next bead in the previous round and the first bead added in the new round [c–d].

4 Continue adding two beads per stitch. As you work, snug up the beads to form a tube, and step up at the end of each round until your rope is the desired length.

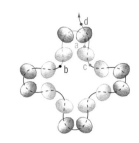

RIGHT-ANGLE WEAVE (RAW)

Flat strip

Step 1 To start a row of right-angle weave, pick up four beads, and tie them into a ring with a square knot. Sew through the first three beads again [fig. 1].

Step 2 Pick up three beads. Sew through the last bead in the previous stitch [fig. 2, a–b], and continue through the first two beads picked up in this stitch [b–c].

Step 3 Continue adding three beads per stitch until the first row is the desired length. You are stitching in a figure-8 pattern, alternating the direction of the thread path for each stitch [fig. 3 and 4].

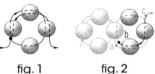

fig. 1   fig. 2

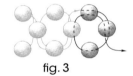

fig. 3

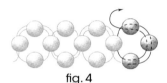

fig. 4

Adding rows in RAW

Step 1 To add a row, sew through the last stitch of row 1, exiting an edge bead along one side.

Step 2 Pick up three beads, and sew through the edge bead your thread exited in the previous step [fig. 5, a–b]. Continue through the first new bead [b–c].

Step 3 Pick up two beads, and sew back through the next edge bead in the previous row and the bead your thread exited at the start of this step [fig. 6, a–b]. Continue through the two new beads and the following edge bead in the previous row [b–c].

Step 4 Pick up two beads, and sew through the last two beads your thread exited in the previous stitch and the first new bead. Continue working a figure-8 thread path, picking up two beads per stitch to complete the row [fig. 7].

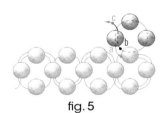

fig. 5

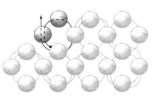

fig. 6

fig. 7

figure

PEYOTE STITCH

Flat even-count peyote

Step 1 Pick up an even number of beads, leaving the desired length tail [figure, a–b]. These beads will shift to form the first two rows as the third row is added.

Step 2 To begin row 3, pick up a bead, skip the last bead added in the previous step, and sew back through the next bead, working toward the tail [b–c]. For each stitch, pick up a bead, skip a bead in the previous row, and sew through the next bead until you reach the first bead picked up in step 1 [c–d]. The beads added in this row are higher than the previous rows and are referred to as "up-beads."

Step 3 For each stitch in subsequent rows, pick up a bead, and sew through the next up-bead in the previous row [d–e]. To count peyote stitch rows, count the total number of beads along both straight edges.

Tubular peyote

Tubular peyote stitch follows the same stitching pattern as flat peyote, but instead of sewing back and forth, you work in rounds.

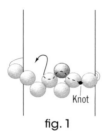

fig. 1

Step 1 Start with an even number of beads knotted into a ring [fig. 1].

Step 2 Sew through the first bead in the ring. Pick up a bead, skip a bead in the ring, and sew through the next bead. Repeat to complete the round.

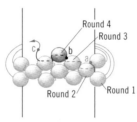

fig. 2

Step 3 To step up to start the next round, sew through the first bead added in round 3 [fig. 2, a–b]. Pick up a bead, and sew through the next bead in round 3 [b–c]. Repeat to achieve the desired length, stepping up after each round.

Circular peyote

Circular peyote is worked in continuous rounds like tubular peyote, but the rounds stay flat and radiate outward from the center as a result of increasing the number of beads per stitch or using larger beads. If the number or size of the beads is not sufficient to fill the spaces between stitches, the circle will not lie flat.

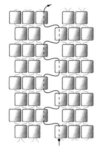

Zipping up

To join two sections of flat peyote stitch invisibly, match up the two pieces so the end rows fit together. "Zip up" the pieces by zigzagging through the up-beads on both ends.

BRICK STITCH

Step 1 To work the typical method, which results in progressively decreasing rows, work the first row in ladder stitch (see "Ladder stitch") to the desired length, exiting the top of the last bead added.

Step 2 Pick up two beads, sew under the thread bridge between the second and third beads in the previous row, and sew back up through the second bead added. To secure this first stitch, sew down through the first bead and back up through the second bead.

Step 3 For the remaining stitches in the row, pick up one bead per stitch, sew under the thread bridge between the next two beads in the previous row, and sew back up through the new bead. The last stitch in the new row will be centered above the last two beads in the previous row, and the new row will be one bead shorter than the previous row.

Increasing: To increase at the start of the row, repeat step 1 above, then repeat step 2, but sew under the thread bridge between the first and second beads in the previous row. To increase at the end of the row, work two stitches off of the thread bridge between the last two beads in the previous row.

SQUARE STITCH

Step 1 String all the beads needed for the first row, then pick up the first bead of the second row. Sew through the last bead of the first row and the first bead of the second row again [**fig. 1**]. Position the two beads side by side so that their holes are parallel.

Step 2 Pick up the next bead of row 2, and sew through the corresponding bead in row 1 and the new bead in row 2 [**fig. 2**]. Repeat across the row.

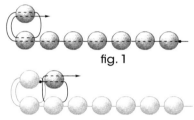

fig. 1

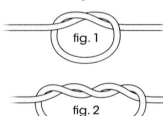

fig. 2

DOUBLE OVERHAND KNOT

For a regular overhand knot, you make a loop with the thread, pass the tail through the loop, and tighten [**fig. 1**].

A double overhand knot creates a fatter and thus more-secure knot. It starts out the same as a regular overhand knot: Make a loop with the thread. Pass the tail through the loop twice [**fig. 2**]. Tighten [**fig. 3**]. Voila! A nice, fat knot with a little more to grab on to.

fig. 1

fig. 2

fig. 3

CRIMPING

Use crimp beads to secure flexible beading wire. Slide the crimp bead into place, and squeeze it firmly with chainnose pliers to flatten it. For a more finished look, use crimping pliers:

Step 1 Position the crimp bead in the hole that is closest to the handle of the crimping pliers. Holding the wires apart, squeeze the pliers to compress the crimp bead, making sure one wire is on each side of the dent [**photo A**].

Step 2 Place the crimp bead in the front hole of the pliers, and position it so the dent is facing the tips of the pliers. Squeeze the pliers to fold the crimp in half [**photo B**]. Tug on the wires to ensure that the crimp is secure.

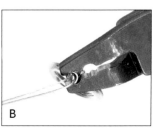

A

B

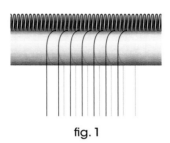

fig. 1

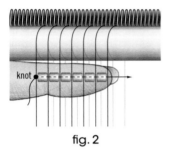

knot

fig. 2

LOOMWORK

Set up the warp: Tie the end of the spool of thread to a screw or hook at the end of the loom. Bring the thread over one spring and across to the spring at the other end of the loom. Wrap the thread around the back of the rod behind the bottom spring and back to the spring at the top of the loom. Wrap the thread between springs, keeping the threads a bead's width apart until you have one more warp thread than the number of beads in the width of the pattern [**fig. 1**]. Keep the tension even, but not too tight. Secure the last warp thread to a hook or screw on the loom, then cut the thread from the spool.

Weave the pattern: Tie the end of 3' of thread to the first warp thread just below the spring at the top of the loom. Bring the needle under the warp threads. String the first row of beads as shown on the pattern and slide them to the knot. Push the beads up between the warp threads with your finger [**fig. 2**]. Sew back through the beads, keeping the needle above the warp threads. Repeat, following the pattern row by row. After you complete the last row, secure the working thread by weaving it into the beadwork.

Gratitude

This book would not be complete if I didn't acknowledge my mama, Ada. She passed her love for handicraft to me by teaching me everything she knew. I've never been bored because I've always had something that I could make with my hands—my mama gave me that ability. By doing this she started a legacy that I will hand on to my children.

My father, Frank, found satisfaction in the simple things: a good horse, a smart dog, and a home-cooked meal.

To my husband, Jeff—you have my utmost love and devotion. To my sons and daughter—Jake, Donnie, and Miranda—I love you to the moon and back.

Afterword

Where do I go from here? I've learned many lessons as I've created this book. I have realized that, as a creative person, my true joy is found smack dab in the middle of making jewelry. The process and system of beading technique is a siren's call that I can't resist. I have my sketchbook and my favorite green pencil. I think I'll go out in the world and look at things. Let's see if I can translate what I see into something made with beads …

About the Author

Beading has been part of Maggie Roschyk's life as far back as she can recall. "I entered a loomed necklace into the Arizona State Fair contest when I was a fourth grader," she says. "I won a ribbon because there weren't any other entrants in my age group."

An artistic mother gave her a head start. "During the long, hot summers growing up in the Southwest, we entertained ourselves by painting, weaving on a large harness loom, making clay pots on a wheel, and beading." As a teenager, she made her own purses and jewelry. Working in libraries as a young mother, she used every lunch hour to pore over reference books on beadwork and spent her precious free time searching for thrift-store jewelry that could be taken apart and made into something new.

In 1995, her mother sent her a package with a note that said: "I think you'll be very interested in what's inside." The package contained the first few issues of a new magazine called *Bead&Button*. "My little world became much larger on that day," Maggie says. From that day on, beadwork and jewelry designing became an integral part of her life. Today Maggie's work can be seen in many publications, including *Bead&Button* magazine and the books *Art Jewelry Today* and *500 Beaded Objects*. Maggie shows her work and teaches at many venues, including the Bead&Button Show in the U.S. and the Bead Art and Jewelry Accessory Fair in Germany. Maggie is a contributing editor to *Bead&Button* and the author of the online column "Maggie's Musings" at Bead&Button.com.

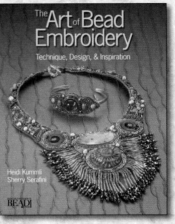
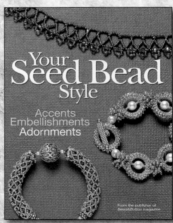

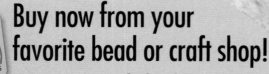